Beautifully Broken

Kimberly Jones-Pothier

authorHOUSE®

AuthorHouse™
1663 Liberty Drive
Bloomington, IN 47403 USA
www.authorhouse.co.uk
Phone: 0800.197.4150

Conquering Hell in High Heels, P.O. Box 142834, Fayetteville, GA 30214

NKJV
Scripture quotations marked NKJV are taken from the New King James Version. Copyright © 1982 by Thomas Nelson, Inc. Used by permission. All rights reserved.

Published by AuthorHouse 04/21/2015

ISBN: 978-1-5049-0339-4 (sc)
ISBN: 978-1-5049-0338-7 (e)

Library of Congress Control Number: 2015906138

Print information available on the last page.

Any people depicted in stock imagery provided by Thinkstock are models, and such images are being used for illustrative purposes only. Certain stock imagery © Thinkstock.

This book is printed on acid-free paper.

Dedication

I would like to dedicate this book
to my first love, God!

To my amazing parents, Drs. Henry and Ann
Jones (Mom and Dad), I love you and couldn't
have hand - picked better parents.

My two amazing sons, Lyncoln and Morgan,
you guys are my life and heartbeat.

And last, but surely not least, my #1, my top priority
for the rest of our lives, Mark. You are the wind in
my sail, my escape, my prize, my joy, best friend
and my love. You are my #SMG, Sexy Man of God! I
love you beyond the moon. Thank you for coming
into my world and showing me what true love
feels like and for being a great example showing
my boys how a man should honor their mom!

Acknowledgements

I'd like to say thank you to:

My mom, Ann Jones, who was my inspiration

throughout this adventure;

Sharenda Williams, who assisted
in editing and contributed

her great ideas;

Onesimus Williams, my executive assistant who

created the book cover and schedules my life.

Contents

Part 2: *my present*

Beautifully broken is where

God does His best work

Part 1

my beginning

simple prayer and you too can experience a total life change:

"Dear God, I am a sinner and need forgiveness. I believe that Jesus Christ shed His precious blood and died for my sin. I am willing to turn from sin. I now invite Christ to come into my heart and life as my personal Savior." Amen.

of cash. After finally understanding that happiness cannot be bought, I came to the end of myself and realized I had no answer except God. Today, I am totally healed, set free and delivered from the feelings of rejection, hopelessness, and brokenness. I am free from the strongholds of my past.

My relationship with God is awesome. I have forgiven my ex-husband and am now married to the absolute man of my dreams! Right now, in this very moment, I am living my life with purpose and passion. For so many of you who share my world through social media and view my posts, what you are witnessing daily in my life is the amazing grace and unconditional love of God. For those of you who do not know my story and never followed me on any social media, you are about to understand the power of God in the life of this beautifully broken woman.

God wants us to love and serve people unconditionally with compassion. In doing this, we will show the love and grace of our God to a lost world. But all the love and service in the world cannot save a person. As much as I want you to read my story and celebrate my deliverance, I want you to have that same personal experience with my Lord Jesus Christ. For all my friends who have never taken that step of faith and invited Jesus Christ into your life as Lord and Savior, we want to give you that opportunity. Just pray this

Introduction

God has graced me with an international ministry across a span of social media sites. Every week I travel and share my testimony of healing and wholeness. God has entrusted me with the assignment of loving people back to life and I am so honored that I have the opportunity to do so daily. I truly believe that hugs heal. Therefore, I make it a point to hug every single person I pray for and mentor.

Many will view my life through foggy lenses and think, "Wow, that girl has really got it all together." The truth is it has not always been that way. Yes, I married the good looking man, had the adorable children and even lived in a 5,000 square feet home. On paper it was the perfect life, but in reality I was miserable.

Having lived through verbal, mental and physical abuse, I became comfortable being the victim of my own story. I lived daily believing that life would be different tomorrow. I poured myself into my design company and thought happiness was a lockbox full

She began dreaming again, allowing God to become the center of her world. For the first time in her life, she went to the Bible to become acquainted with the One who was now healing her from the inside out. Kimberly became consumed by the process of understanding her purpose and getting completely free.

As we now watch God unfold His will in Kimberly's life, even we are amazed at how God not only restores all that the cankerworm has stolen but gives back more than we can even contain. Seeing our daughter not only fulfilled in the ways of the Lord but highly blessed in marriage humbles us as we cover and support her purpose, *loving people back to life.*

Love, Dad and Mom

for those areas in which she was lacking to excel in others. Even as a high school student, Kimberly was ordering her world.

No one would ever have guessed that Kimberly was fighting with low self-esteem and insecurities. Even after marriage, it looked like she had life all figured out. When Kimberly's world came crashing down and we received that call for help, we knew that our independent daughter was in dire need to have reached outside to invite us into her private world.

One of the hardest times for a parent is to see your child hurting and know you can only hold them. You cannot heal that broken heart. After Kimberly and her boys moved back to our home, it was heartbreaking as we overheard our little girl, now a mature woman, sobbing herself to sleep at night. The greatest solace for us was that she and the boys were safe in our home. We would allow the process of healing to work no matter how long it took.

We knew God had a plan for Kimberly. We had spoken this word over her life since she was born so nothing would deter her in that journey of purpose. Watching God unveil His plan as Kimberly moved through the metamorphosis of change was one of the most refreshing times of our lives. She had returned home broken with no idea what tomorrow would hold besides the future years to come.

Foreword

As we knelt together that dusky evening, Henry and I gave our request to God. We traveled fulltime in evangelism with our two-year-old son, Rob, and we knew we wanted a little girl to complete our family. I wanted a blue-eyed blonde (like me) and Henry wanted that little brown-eyed girl. But most of all, we wanted our little baby to be all that God designed.

Because we were evangelists, Ann went home to her mom's to give birth as I continued traveling the last month. Who could have known that two days after Ann arrived home, our little girl would decide it's time to be born. When I got to the hospital nine hours after birth, I held our 5 lb. 2 oz. Kimberly in my arms and gave her to God.

As Kimberly was growing up, we knew she was one of a kind. Because she was challenged in school, we began to understand the importance of encouragement in every area of her life. Little did we realize how, in her young life, she would compensate

one

A Young Girl and Shattered Dreams

My Beginning

God, church and family, most days this was the complete order of my life. Born into a family of preachers, my entry into ministry was almost inevitable. Prior to serving as local pastors my parents were full time evangelists, preaching, praying, and singing throughout the entire United States and later in many Muslim dominated countries. Laboring not in vain, they have witnessed thousands of people experiencing salvation, healing and deliverance all over the world.

With the arrival of my brother and me, their ministry continued without hindrance. When I was born, my brother was two years old. Mom and Dad were in the midst of a revival. Mom went home to give birth while my dad continued evangelizing. Two days later my mom went into labor and my dad hurried home to be with us. It was not very long before we were all on the road evangelizing as a family. With two toddlers and a blossoming ministry, stopping or slowing down was never an option. Instead, we were right there with them.

We traveled across America, sitting in churches and tent revivals, spending weeks at a time in one city. Church attendance and participation was very important to the Jones family. Even as we grew into teenagers, the thought of missing church for any reason never entered our minds. Again, if Mom and Dad were there, so were we.

The Joneses were always seen together. Even if our parents went out for the evening, we would go with them. As a child, I remember my parents being very selective of my influencers. Honestly, my brother and I never had a babysitter. Mom and Dad had to approve the kids we played with and I would often become very agitated with them. My parents always provided me a safe place to call home and protected me from anything that would cause me harm, especially other people.

Not discounting the personal struggles I encountered, my childhood was not typical but it was great. Our everyday life was unusual to some but there were moments we did normal things. One of my fondest memories is driving fourteen hours to spend Christmas with my grandparents. My grandmother, whom we affectionately called Mawmaw, would cook for hours in preparation of our arrival. Her desire was for us all to enjoy our favorite foods. In my mind, I knew as long as I had the love of my parents and grandparents, life would be perfect.

As I look back I wonder how I could ever become so broken and distant from God. Even as a child, Satan was trying to steal my future by causing me to focus on the temporary instead of the eternal. Feelings of anger, shame and rejection began to manifest. We were a musical family and every night I would fall asleep listening to my favorite bands playing on a radio that was tucked under the covers because I did not like gospel music.

Jolted awake one morning at seven o'clock with worship music blaring throughout our home, I was furious. There was no place to go to get rid of this music. My dad had connected speakers throughout our home and I had lost control of this situation. This occurrence, however, did not stop my attempts at full control of my life and decisions.

Chosen Child

Most assured that I did not want to go to hell, at the age of seven I asked Jesus into my heart and was baptized. Not at all interested in the sort of spiritual experience my parents had, I thought just getting saved was enough. Trusting my parents to always be there for me even after making the poorest decisions, I had placed the burden of my natural and spiritual care on my parents. Yes, I had asked Jesus to save me but I had never pursued a personal and fruitful relationship with Him. Nor did I acknowledge His love or wisdom.

For many years I heard my daddy and other preachers talk about this amazing God and His unconditional love for us. After sitting through years of religious instruction in Sunday School and youth meetings, incorrectly I thought this kind of love was only reserved for the "good" Christian. If you ask me to explain why this preacher's kid was so trivial in spiritual things I could not give you a satisfactory answer.

However, in my heart, I always knew God needed or better yet, He wanted to be at the center of my life. He had a plan for my life that was finalized before I was ever born but I was so easily distracted by my desire to become a success. Choosing instead to do things that were contrary to His will and moving farther and farther away from God, I could not see His divine hand keeping me protected. As a result, my journey through life took me down a road filled with potholes of hurt, dangerous curves of habits and multiple speed bumps of heartache. Truly I had created my own storms and got mad at God when it rained.

Religious Restriction

Spend one hour with me and you will know that I absolutely hate religion and all of its man-made rules and guidelines. Religion can leave people injured and it places God in a box limiting what He is capable of doing in and through you. My parents were influential members of an organization that restricted women from using their gifts in ministry. Taught to sing or be silent, God said otherwise and I felt a tug in my heart to preach the word of God.

Some days I would spend hours singing and preaching to my Barbie dolls. One afternoon, at the age of four, my mom overheard me saying, "My daddy doesn't believe in women preachers, so I guess I will just have to sing." It was as though I thought I had to discard one gift and settle for functioning in the other. But God had a specific plan for my life.

For I know the thoughts that I think toward
you, says the Lord, thoughts of peace and
not of evil, to give you a future and a hope.
(Jeremiah 29:11)

Satan is such a loser! In an attempt to discredit the call of God on my life, Satan always reminded me of my struggle with memorization and the inability to retain information. He would constantly tell me you are nothing, you are a failure. He always tries to manipulate what God has said to us about us. The most dangerous weapon he uses is six inches between our ears, the mind. When he can get inside our head and change or control our thinking and thought patterns, we will miss everything God has already said about us because of a momentary distraction. Now I have learned to be less concerned about what Satan says about me and more focused on what God has ordained for me. No longer was I going to settle!

Once I accepted this call on my life to preach, I had to get into position to hear His voice clearly about my future and what He had for me. No longer was I listening to the reason why I could not, but for the first time I was hearing all the reason why

MY DADDY DOESN'T BELIEVE IN WOMEN PREACHERS, SO I GUESS I WILL JUST HAVE TO SING.

I had to walk in my purpose. My future was not limited to just singing but God had ordained me to be a heart healer. Now I travel the world singing and preaching. All the glory belongs to Him. I just get to reap the reward and the benefits.

My discontentment with religion did not stop then. At a very pivotal moment in our family and my parents' ministry, I observed church people mistreating my mom and dad. Hearing my mom weeping because of the rejection she had experienced by the people who supposedly loved them was a memory I was not going to soon forget. Witnessing this terrible tragedy happen to the most loving people on the planet bothered me and as a consequence, I carried the resentment for people and religion into all of my relationships.

Deal with that Devil

During the traumatic times in our childhood, we were open to the still small voices of evil spirits. When we heard them, we thought they were our own thoughts, since we had no wisdom yet to consider otherwise. The demonic forces plants feelings of rejection, causing us to become shameful and self-rejection, self-hatred, and bitterness are then produced.

Then the spirits set up a protective mechanism against these feelings, usually in the form of blame shifting. Inadvertently, becoming blind to our faults and the unveiling of our true feelings seems to only bring us more shame. For this cause we hold our feelings inside and learn to act like nothing others say or do really bothers us. As a teenager I would say, "When I grow up, no one will tell me what to do." These very words set the direction of my life and became a hidden agenda into adulthood.

The Lord had given my parents wisdom on how to deal with me and my lack of respect for the things of God. The way in which they handled the music was ingenious and done with wisdom that came only through prayer and fasting. God had shown them how to deal with the problem spiritually. My parents were not reactive, instead they became proactive. They did not fight me in the physical but in the spiritual.

Mom and Dad knew there was a unique gifting and calling upon my life. When they set those speakers up in the house and played worship music, it was not for my present but it was a setup for my future. The Bible tells us to not be ignorant concerning the wiles of the enemy. They both recognize the enemy was after their baby girl and he was not going to have her without a fight.

They recognized Satan and his schemes and tactics, now so do I. Anything that is contrary to the Word of God was assigned to assassinate me and my dream.

The Bible is full of promises to refute the lies of the enemy. God also has given us spiritual weapons to fight against these spiritual attacks on our emotions. With these weapons I take authority over my emotions daily. I am fighting for my family and you, my awesome friends. I do not fight against my flesh but those spirits that try to rule and reign in my life.

> For we wrestle not against flesh and blood,
> but against principalities, against powers,
> against the rulers of the darkness of this
> world, against spiritual wickedness in high
> places. (Ephesians 6:12)

We are more than conquerors in Christ Jesus. No longer will I allow the enemy to cause me to settle for anything less than the best of what God has planned for me! The power of God lives on the inside of me and I can speak my divinely designed future into existence.

> "For all have sinned and fall short of the
> glory of God, being justified freely by His
> grace through the redemption that is in
> Christ Jesus." (Romans 3:23-24)

Saved by Grace Not Works

To our family, being saved had always been about works and how we appeared to those who were members of our organization. If you looked and acted holy enough, you would go to heaven. If you had no desire to wear makeup, jewelry, or slacks, you were accepted by your fellow brothers and sisters in Christ. The security of our salvation existed almost solely in our appearances. Acting and looking holy enough was your ticket to heaven.

At a conference I heard a pastor describing the men and women who were actively part of our organization. He stated that the men looked like they had stepped out of Esquire magazine but they ugly up their wives. My mom really did look older than Dad because she always wore her hip-length hair piled up on her head. Even so, my mom never complained and was a true example of a godly wife.

When I was fifteen, after much prayer and intense study, my dad introduced the message of grace to our family. Prior to disrupting our holiness lifestyle, dad spent countless hours studying the Bible and he read an innumerable amount of books by authors who had researched the importance of grace in a Christian's life. Soon he understood more and more of Paul's teachings in the New Testament on the works of the flesh and how we cannot live well enough or work hard enough to earn God's forgiveness.

He recognized that we could only be made righteous by what Jesus Christ did for us when He took our sins in His body to the cross. He had seen many leading with double standards. They would leave their religion and all its legalistic standards at home when they went on vacation. However, my parents always made sure that what we professed publicly is what we lived privately. So after weeks of prayer and research, Dad taught us this most important Biblical subject. He summarized grace as the divine love and protection bestowed freely on people.

We were trying to fully understand the grace message. My dad, the prolific and wise orator that he is, thoroughly explained how we could never live holy enough to be saved. He helped us to understand the purpose of Jesus, Calvary and the cross. I remember a vacation in Florida when we met a family from one of our local churches. They looked totally different on vacation because they were not dressed according to the church guidelines. They were so nervous when they saw us and began apologizing for their looks. What a Bible lesson for us as my dad showed us grace on that day. He told that family that we were so happy to see them and he loved them no matter how they dressed.

One evening a family meeting was called. Mom and Dad discussed and announced their intentions of leaving the organization in which they had been faithful members for many years. Because our organization did not teach about grace, my parents knew that we would be unequally yoked if we remained as members. They always cooperated with the belief system of the group and would never have brought dissension by staying actively involved in leadership positions while knowing in their hearts that they believed differently. This decision proved to be a pivotal and life changing moment for our family that not only affected them but my brother and me also.

My mom had always been a devoted wife to my father. She was a woman who lived in complete submission to her husband and lived according to the beliefs of our church. When our standards of holiness began to shift, I watched my mom go through months of indecision and introspection. For eighteen years, my mom had not worn make-up, cut her hair, worn jewelry or slacks. The mark of a dedicated Christian woman in our organization at that time was to be seen and not heard. She was a silent bystander and wife.

After submitting to this lifestyle for so many years, this would be a life altering change and she wanted to hear the voice of God to know that all of these changes aligned with the word of God. Her only desire was to be found pleasing in the sight of God. She was finding a true, personal relationship with Jesus Christ for herself. Looking back today, I now know that the Christian woman who emerged after this monumental lifestyle change fell in love with the Word of God and determined to only be led by the Spirit and not the traditions of men. As a woman, I respect her desire to hear God.

The ultimate game changer during that season for our family was on Valentine's Day. Our dad bought my mom wedding rings. His gift was bittersweet for all of us because we had never before been allowed to wear any kind of jewelry. My mom realized that this would be an outward sign that we truly were changing. This one gesture, that so many consider to be routine, was momentous to the introduction of our new life under grace. The decision to embrace the message of grace would not only affect the Jones family, but thousands of men and women who would need my father for spiritual covering and mentoring.

We had only lived one way and it was according to very strict guidelines. We lived by the Articles of Faith of our church and knew, to stay in good standing with our organization, we could not deviate from any of the teachings. My parents did not allow us to watch television. I still remember my mother checking up on me as I played with my neighbor's children. She knew I would yield to the temptation of watching their television if given the opportunity. The day that a television was brought into our home is still a memorable event in my life. Because of the lack of a television, my brother and I became captivated by it. Even then, my parents set guidelines as to what programs we would watch and when. The world as I had known it for so long was quickly changing and the process was not easy. For the first time I was allowed to cut my hair, wear short sleeves and even pants. I remember being thankful that I was now able to fit in and look more like my friends.

The most difficult time for our family as my parents led our church was to see families that we dearly loved leaving because they could not accept the grace message. They would tell my dad that he was the greatest pastor anyone could have but they could not change. One of the deacons even looked across the desk at my dad and told him that the bank was going to own the building, and there was no way the church could succeed with the grace message. As a teenager, I watched as people left and I took it personally. I did not understand how my parents could not only love these people but also bless them as they left. Another great example of grace to me was seeing my parents love people, expecting nothing in return. Of course the bank never owned the church and today my brother has three services on Sunday at that location. God is good!

All the changes brought even more confusion into my life. For so many years we were taught that doing these things would send us to hell, but now they were just accepted? Often I questioned the assumptions of our religion. My mind and heart were a jumbled mess. My uncertainty about how the message of grace would impact my life put the fear of going to hell inside of me. But instead of leaning toward God for guidance, direction and understanding just as my mom had, I was drawn away by my own desires and enticed (James 1:14) by destructive behaviors and attitudes.

The rejection I had felt for so long wasn't someone necessarily wanting me out of their lives, but someone God needed out of my future.

two

Don't Live Out Your Labels

My Labels

Learning Disabled

Religion was only one in a series of things leading to my life of dysfunction. Being labeled by my teachers and strangers in the second grade as Learning Disabled, I was placed in a special education class because of my inability to retain information and difficulty with phonics. Subsequently, because of this diagnosis, mom and dad enrolled me in several different Christian schools with hopes of finding the right school to accommodate my disability.

As I was sitting in a special needs classroom, I saw visible signs of the other students' respective disabilities but my outside looked normal. "Where was mine?" I would ask myself. Often I would stand in front of the mirror feeling my face, thinking and saying, "Maybe I am drooling. Maybe I am special. Maybe I just don't know it." The observable evidence of my learning disability was the incorrect pronunciation of the word *beautiful.* I would say *boo-tiful.*

Although there were no tangible signs of my disability, the emotional scars were there. The brokenness I felt on the inside held me hostage to the label that had been placed on me at such a young age. Of course, the stigma of being in special education classes began to wreak havoc on my frame of mind.

Six years of Learning Disability classes caused me to feel ashamed and I began to sink into isolation and allowed insecurity to rule me. The enemy was having a great time keeping me a prisoner within myself. "Nothing is wrong with me," that is what I would tell myself daily, but I did not feel normal. All of my peers would remain in the general education classes while I was isolated and placed in a smaller class. Leaving the classroom would cause an immediate feeling of embarrassment to come upon me. Being away from my friends and them knowing I struggled with learning, I hated going to those classes. All I wanted was to be like my peers.

My brother excelled academically and found learning to be a breeze. During this time, I felt so alone in my struggle. Who could understand my pain? What was so wrong with me that I would have to be faced with all of these challenges? My mom and I would spend hours together at night studying, only for me to wake up the next morning unable to recall any of the information. When it was time for the tests, I still could not recall anything that we had studied the entire week or the previous night.

Can you imagine the frustrations that I faced, not to mention my mom as well? She would spend hours with me reviewing and rehearsing words, only to find out that I had failed yet another exam. This proved to be an emotionally stressful period for us both. The pain of my learning disability led me down a path of merely learning to cope with my dysfunction. Overcoming it was difficult; in fact, it had become my new normal.

Labels you don't have to wear

The moment you meet someone new, labeling begins. You're rebellious or you're shy. Even in job interviews we are asked to label ourselves with the famous question, "Name three words that describe you." I remember church members talking about me to my dad. "Kim is rebellious. She treated my daughter badly." As people criticized me, my dad would dispute these labels and tell me what an amazing daughter I was. He knew I was full of introspection and he never allowed anyone to put me in that box of shame. Of course my dad knew that I was busy judging myself so he made sure I was protected and free from criticism.

Labels take away our value and limit our potential. They replace our true identity in Christ with false identities. When you allow your labels to identify who you are, then you are functioning within the confines of the label. Get to know who you are in Christ.

I will praise you, for I am fearfully and
wonderfully made; (Psalm 139:14)

While preaching, I often reference the story of the man with the withered hand in Mark 3:1-5. He had been born this way and never saw it as a disability or a dysfunction. It was just who he was, the man with the withered hand. It was his total identity. A conversation about him would only identify his disability rather than his ability. One can only wonder what his neighbors called him. Can you imagine the references he not only made about himself but heard from others also? His name was not even listed in the Bible.

Calling him on the phone would be quite interesting. He probably answered, "The man with the withered hand speaking." That is exactly how so many of us answer our phones, texts and emails; the woman who was raped, the man who was molested or the divorced Christian.

The assignment on my life leads me to so many injured people. Often I meet men and women who have been abused physically and/or sexually. They struggle with trust, rejection and abandonment. Because they have been mishandled or mistreated, they tend to keep everyone they meet at a safe distance. It never baffles me when women say they have lived in a private hell because of what their father did to them in the middle of the night or the physical abuse they suffer at the hands of their spouse. Personally, I have lived in my own private hell for a very long time. You become prisoner to your own way of stinking thinking.

Some people wear self-imposed labels. When they look in the mirror all they see is that vulnerable little girl or that quiet boy who couldn't tell anyone what happened. They carry the feeling of being dirty everywhere they go; to school, to work and, most dreadfully, to church. Contrary to what most believe, being saved does not erase the pain or the memory of what happened to you. It instead gives you a place of safety to walk out forgiveness.

As long as I was dancing to my own beat, forgiveness was not a part of the routine. It was not an option but now it is my only option. In the presence of God, His mind changed my actions. This transformed and renewed mind gives me permission to move forward and I refuse to look back.

You are only who or what you answer to and who you are is not what you have done or what was done to you. When you know who God has called you to be, you will not answer to anything less than that name. No longer answer to what happened to you because God has called you His. We are His children and He is our Father.

Like so many who are in denial about their brokenness, when the man with the withered hand was asked to stretch out his hand by the healer, he probably stretched out his good hand. To him, that withered hand was normal. He had learned to just cope. More than likely he had everything built to suit his handicap. If he drove, the car would have been designed for a driver with a withered hand. His home probably would have featured amenities that would be just what a man like him required. He would visit others and think, "Man, they are strange.

Coping means "to face and deal with responsibilities, problems, or difficulties, especially successfully or in a calm or adequate manner." Just like the man with the withered hand and me, many of you have created and mastered the strategies for coping. You don't know how to fix it so you learn how to just live with the handicap, pain, problem and dysfunction. After all this is normal, right?

My experiences then were like many of yours today. Willing to make the necessary sacrifice to no longer be trapped by those labels, my method for staying free is by any means necessary. I refuse to wear those labels ever again even if I have to lay hands on my head, saying to those spirits of insecurity and shame, "Come out."

If you are facing a situation that you cannot seem to find a way out by yourself, you can turn it over to God. You probably feel as though you have hit a wall in life and cannot go any farther. Not only can David run through a troop and leap over a wall, but so can you and me.

> For by thee I have run through a troop: by
> my God have I leaped over a wall.
> (II Samuel 22:30)

Being labeled as Learning Disabled was an obstacle I had to endure. It was a challenge that I had to live with but now my testimony is that "I can do all things through Christ who strengthens me." (Philippians 4:13).

Do not allow the labels to limit your potential. Conquering these obstacles in life can seem impossible, but with God all things are possible.

> Yet in all these things we are more than
> conquerors through Him who loved us.
> (Romans 8:37)

You need to spend time reading and listening to encouraging words. Whenever I feel like those labels are starting to be attached to me again, I get alone and spend time in the presence of God. Take authority over the labels. Begin to decree and declare, "I am more than a conqueror. I am the head and not the tail, the lender and not the borrower. I am above and not beneath. I am who God says I am. He says I am healed and I am no longer a victim but a victor. His Word is truth and He cannot lie!

Pretty Girl, Party Animal

The first day of tenth grade, my appearance was so altered that my closest friends did not recognize me. It was almost like a new student had entered our school in my body. New clothes, a new hairstyle and makeup, everything about me had been changed. My popularity increased so I decided to run for student government.

After being elected as a class officer, my life became a whirlwind of activities. Whatever I wanted, I could just go after it and achieve it. At least that is what I believed. Addicted to the attention, I realized the power of a pretty girl and started to use 'Kimberly power'. My reputation for being the party animal grew quickly and I always had friends lined up waiting for me to go out and party. Not yet legally licensed to drive, I never lacked plans on Friday nights or any evening during the week for that matter.

On the outside I had it all together but on the inside my heart was still bruised and damaged. My lack of love for myself had followed me into high school. After so many years, I was still carrying the baggage of insecurity and low self-esteem along with the label of Learning Disability. Add to this the religious confusion that was still attached to me and things were slowly becoming unmanageable.

I tried to pull things together but I continued to spin a web of bad decisions and heartache. In that season of my life, I had become more of a follower and not the leader that God had purposed for me and I was becoming more and more disrespectful to my parents. My mom and dad had a strict zero tolerance policy for disrespect and disobedience but I was constantly pushing the boundaries seeing how far I could go.

One afternoon I had been instructed to come home immediately following school but instead I chose to disobey. My then best friend, and greatest influencer at the time, and I were involved in a near fatal car accident. While I was being transported by ambulance to the local hospital, my friend had to be transported by life flight to a trauma center. She had sustained a life altering brain injury.

After several hours, my parents were allowed to take me home but my friend was not so fortunate. She was admitted to the hospital and for more than six weeks my dad would go to the intensive care unit to pray over my friend and her mom. It was quickly evident that she would never be the same.

The enemy made several attempts on that day to take me out, but God said, "No." During the time we were waiting for the emergency vehicles to arrive on the scene of our accident, I began to have a seizure. God sent a Good Samaritan to assist and keep me stable during this episode.

Surviving the most terrifying afternoon of my life was proof that my parents were always covering me in prayer. My parents had already walked through so many life altering experiences with me and now potential death. They always showered me with their unconditional love and acceptance. God had answered their prayers for me and my friend, sparing our lives. For some, this experience would have urged them to change, but I was independently stubborn and continued down that same path of rebellion and self-destruction.

On my sixteenth birthday my parents prepared an impressive party. They had invited all my friends and spent the entire afternoon grilling and decorating. My parade of friends arrived and after thirty minutes they were ready to move on to the next party. Of course, being the party girl, I was expected to accompany them.

My parents refused to let me leave the house that evening, and I was forced to spend my sixteenth birthday at home with my family. Only one of my friends stayed back with me, but I was so infuriated about not being able to do what I wanted that I spent the entire night spewing about the unfairness of my parents.

My mom would always say, "We're making memories." Didn't she know that this was the most important night of my life? I was thinking, "Ugh, don't we have enough memories? I have an image to keep up and being here is not helping me do that."

Paul writes, "When I was a child, I spoke as a child, I understood as a child, I thought as a child; but when I became a (wo)man, I put away childish things" (1 Corinthians 13:11). In retrospect, the tough love shown by my parents that night has helped me to become the strong woman I am today. However, in that moment, I would rather have been anywhere in the world other than at home.

Allowing my challenges to dictate my life, I thought if I could just change schools and my environment, then everything would be better. After all, this method of insanity had worked in the past. So at my request I transferred to a different high school in the eleventh grade. After changing schools, I had new friends and for a while things seemed to be getting better.

After getting my license, I wanted a car. My brother had a horrible mustard yellow compact car and my parents gave it to me. There was no way I was going to be seen driving that car. Trying to make me happy, they decided to buy me a red Camaro. For most teenage girls that would be a dream come true, but I was a BMW girl.

Desperate to get the car I wanted, I decided to get a job so I could buy my own car. Shortly thereafter I found the perfect car. It was a steel gray BMW. Without any money from my dad or mom, I purchased my dream car. It was the most liberating experience of my teenage life.

Temporarily, I felt like a million dollars driving to high school in the car I had purchased. This major milestone started my transition into becoming a burgeoning independent woman. Because I had experienced so many failures and disappointments, doing something like purchasing my own car with my own money was monumental. All the confusing times and changes in my life suddenly did not matter because, for the first time, I proved to myself and others I was capable of being successful.

After this experience, I felt there was nothing I could not do. It was a time of independence when I thought I knew exactly what I wanted and how to obtain it. Who could tell me what to do now? Things were starting to look up for me. A high school student working full time and driving my BMW to school, yes, I had arrived!

Miracles are easy to get but hard to keep, I think deliverance is the same

three

Twice Married ... The Wrong Way

My Happily Never After

Despite the difficulty of learning, I completed high school with a vocational certificate in cosmetology. Overcoming challenges had become my great motivator, but after completing the greatest challenge of all I quickly became bored with my life as it was. My favorite saying was, "I'm bored! ...Bored with work, church, family, and life. Just bored...!"

Soon after high school, contrary to the wishes and concerns of my parents, I decided to marry, attempting to dispel my boredom. For me, being married seemed like the appropriate solution to all my problems, so at eighteen I got married.

We received no counsel and would not allow anyone to speak into our lives. Eighteen and in love with love, we moved out of the country and for the first time in my life I came face-to-face with being alone. Since I had never quite mastered the idea of being by myself, I was absolutely terrified. There was no family around and my typically large social circle had become a party of one.

Fourteen months later the infatuation was over and so was the marriage. After informing my parents that I wanted to get a divorce, they supported my decision but explained that they had given me the most extravagant wedding and were not willing to pay for the divorce also.

One year prior to this decision, my husband and I had moved to the northeast United States and I had become deeply involved in a mega ministry. Now I realize that staying busy in church does not solve those problems that you live with daily. It takes both parties in a marriage to see major change. My pastor and friend counseled me and said it would take both of us to make this marriage work. Evident that we both were not committed to making the marriage work, I wanted out. Determined to move on with my life, I filed for divorce.

Five months after my divorce I was at the altar again making the same promises I had made the first time, but I just knew this time would be different. We had met in a church and ministry setting, surely this was going to be my happily ever after. Not surprisingly, my endless cycle of brokenness ensued. Our life together was the true definition of insanity, doing the same thing over and over again but expecting different results.

True happiness, a happy marriage and a happy life, that was all I had ever really desired. In my mind, I had equated this type of happiness with the love and acceptance of a natural man. However, in reality, the kind of love I craved could only come from God. The God I heard my dad preach about, He is the only One who could love me unconditionally. Until now, what I did not understand was that only God could repair the brokenness I felt on the inside. Unless that place becomes healed and whole, you will continue to fill it with more and more broken pieces of other things.

How foolish of me to think this marriage would be different when I had followed a similar pattern. Still in love with being in love, we had no premarital counseling. We were adults who thought we knew what we wanted and what we were doing. Both of us had years of unresolved unforgiveness from our childhood that had attracted us to one another. Wholeheartedly, I believe you attract who you are, not what you want. Let me just tell you, I was broken and that is exactly what came my way.

He was an absolutely gorgeous musician and singer. We both had come from strong religious backgrounds but we did not have a true and real relationship with God. Our gifts had opened doors that allowed us to sing before thousands of people in mega churches all over the nation.

One afternoon, concerned for my future and wanting to dissuade my decision to get married again so quickly, daddy took me out for a drive on one of the busiest highways in Georgia, Interstate 285. You might be thinking, "Why that particular highway?" Let me explain this highway to you just in case you have not experienced its architectural ingenuity. This interstate bypass wraps around the entire metropolitan city of Atlanta and literally leads everywhere and nowhere at the same time. It is simply just a series of access points and interchanges. If you never exit then you will drive in circles.

YOU ATTRACT WHO YOU ARE, NOT WHAT YOU WANT!

He expressed his many concerns to me and likened my future to the never ending cycle of this highway. As we were driving around he began to say, "Baby, you need to get healed from the pain of the past before you can move into the next season of your life." I appreciated his concern and care, but remember, I knew what I wanted. We were married and that decision has caused my family and me years of turmoil, pain and confusion. God is not the author of confusion; He is a God of order and peace. Paul speaks about the peace I so desired to have in my life.

> And the peace of God, which surpasses all
> understanding, will guard your hearts and
> minds through Christ Jesus. (Philippians 4:7)

My sincerest desire was to have this peace. Instead, my life was full of chaotic decision-making and ungodliness. Protecting me and my heart had become my agenda. Not allowing God to be the complete authority in my life had set me up for many struggles. The enemy had me believing I could make it in my own strength and I began to feel invincible.

Eleven months after we married, our first son Morgan arrived and two years later our second son Lyncoln was born. They were the most perfect little beings and brought great joy to our lives and marriage. Those two boys were the most loved babies on the planet by both their parents. Finally I was getting my happy ending; at least that's what I thought.

We were offered an amazing opportunity to serve as worship leaders in a mega ministry thousands of miles from home. Although we missed being close to relatives, it was a great fit for our family. And for the first time, quite possibly the only time, we had a normal marriage. Everything was as it should be in a picturesque marriage, I was a stay-at-home mom raising our beautiful boys. We were building great relationships, leading praise and worship, and our kids were attending church.

As we all know, the enemy cannot stand for us to be living in our purpose and according to the will of God. After eleven months of bliss, our lives changed forever. We were presented an opportunity that would allow us to be closer to both our families. Surely this was divinely designed by God.

However, without seeking God for wisdom and direction, we packed up our kids and moved back across the country, and the harmony we once shared met its expiration date. We had decided to make a move that would set us up for years of emotional pain and heartache. To the outside world we looked like the perfect couple. In reality what was once our holy matrimony turned into unholy discord and the cycle of dysfunction was started again. Welcome to "Interstate 285," also known as our life.

The marriage became tumultuous and yet God continued to open great doors and opportunity in business and ministry for us. After we relocated, I started an interior design firm that became financially lucrative but introduced me to many types of lifestyles. More than seventy percent of the job was getting clients and attending high profile parties.

Be that as it may, we did not understand how important respect was in a marriage. Both of us lived in anger and bitterness from our respective pasts. We were living a nightmare that was masqueraded as a fairy tale. The only thing most people saw was my beautiful home, designer clothes and bags, fancy cars and ten-carat diamond.

We looked the part, but behind closed doors, our marriage was in shambles. We were two broken people trying to become whole while continuing to tear each other apart. We fought each other constantly and subjected our boys to violent outbursts and name-calling. This is the life we had chosen and it was a sixteen-year journey filled with deceitfulness, abuse, alcoholism and dysfunction. How could we have ever allowed our sweet boys to live in that kind of toxic environment?

Successful in business but I was a failure in life. Refusing to submit to my spouse, I had to be in control so no one else could hurt me. No one was going to be in charge of my decisions but me. Why should I allow anyone else to make decisions for me? As the breadwinner for our family, I felt that I had earned the privilege of maintaining my control. The spirit of control had consumed my very existence.

I owned a lockbox with thousands of dollars in cash that I kept in my possession at all times. As long as I had cash I could buy whatever was needed to bring me happiness. Wow, how foolish was I to think I could purchase the happiness I craved. Happiness is a temporary situation. Buying a new car or house or even a new dress gives you short-term happiness. However, what God offers to give you is that joy that surpasses all understanding.

While shopping one afternoon I lost consciousness and collapsed. This incident set me up for months of fear and anxiety. The doctors had no explanation as to why I would experience sudden blackouts and terrible headaches. Although I was not spiritually minded at the time, when the doctors could offer no explanation, I could recognize Satan's attack and knew how to respond. At that moment I told myself I would be prepared to do battle when those attacks returned.

SIN WILL TAKE YOU FARTHER THAN YOU WANT TO GO, KEEP YOU LONGER THAN YOU WANT TO STAY AND COST YOU MORE THAN YOU WANT TO PAY.

Mom and Dad had raised me to understand the healing power of Jesus Christ and taught me to apply

His blood in spiritual warfare. Revelation 12:11 tells us that the servants of God overcame Satan by the blood of the Lamb and by the word of their testimony, and they did not love their lives to the death. You will overcome Satan when you testify personally to what the Word of God says the blood of Jesus does for you.

> Much more then, having now been justified
> by His blood, we shall be saved from wrath
> through Him. (Romans 5:9)

Pleading the blood delivers provision for every need, including inner healing, finances, physical healing, deliverance and wisdom. When pleading the blood of Jesus, you appropriate, apply, declare, proclaim and put your trust in the completed work of His shed blood. You may use whatever words you are comfortable with, however, the expression, "In Jesus Name, I plead the blood over (name your condition)" is powerful.

Even in my brokenness, I knew that the name of Jesus gave me guaranteed victory because, "no weapon that is formed against me shall prosper" (Isaiah 54:17) and "Yet in all these things we are more than conquerors through Him who loved us" (Romans 8:37). Of course, just because we have defeated the enemy once does not mean he will not try us again. He has tried me subsequently in different ways only to be defeated over and over again.

Recognize that Satan has power to come against us but, he can only touch us if we give him the authority. Jesus took Satan's authority when He set the captives free at Calvary and is now standing at the right hand of the Father in Heaven. Remember, Satan does not have the authority over you. Just having this knowledge will truly change everything in your life.

One day, while showering I felt the headache and uneasiness returning. Immediately, I began spiritual warfare, calling on the name of Jesus. My husband walked in and I said to him, "Either pray or get out!" He quickly left the room and I continued praying until I knew I was healed. Since that day, I have been free and never again experienced that type of an attack on my body.

Sin will take you farther than you want to go, keep you longer than you want to stay and cost you more than you want to pay. My dad always told me to mark the paths of those who have gone before us so we do not make the same mistakes. Experience is the best teacher, but there is a substitute teacher known as *Observation*. As you can see, I still was not ready to adhere to his great advice and wisdom.

Because I was no threat to Satan, he left me to my devices. However today I am healed, whole and pulling others out of the clinches of his influence. He dare not mess with me. My prayer, praise and worship dispel the hand of the enemy in the lives of men and women across the world. I am a world changer and a history maker and when I wake up in the mornings he gets nervous.

Everything that was working against me has turned and is now working in my favor. "I know that all things are working together for my good" (Romans 8:28). Yes, that includes the good, the bad and most definitely, the ugly. I can testify that even when I don't deserve it, God is faithful. He never left me in my mess. God said, "Kim, you did that and you are going to do this but I am still going to use you!"

The Beginning of the End

Much like the prodigal son in Luke 15:11-32, I left home thinking I could handle life away from my father's house. For a while I did well but there was a day of reckoning when I had a pig pen experience.

We had a beautiful home in a gated community. After being absent for a while, my husband returned and an argument ensued that forced me out of our house. In the middle of the night, partially dressed, I found myself lying in between the shrubs and my large home. Barefoot with no cell phone and my kids sleeping upstairs, I knew we could not stay in this toxic environment any longer. It was time for a change, but change involves choice.

For the first time in a long time I had a clear mind and knew what needed to happen. My kids deserved better and I realized I was worth better. Lying there, because I did not want to go anywhere without my two boys, I cried out to God and He comforted this little girl that had been filled with so much hatred and anger.

At daybreak, I reentered my home that had been a war zone the previous evening. After checking in on my boys, I began listening to praise and worship music. My desire was to find my way back to God and to recondition my spirit for the things of God. I knew I needed to leave but hesitated one more time and continued taking the same path hoping things would change.

The turning point came a few weeks later as we were returning home from a friend's house. There was a violent outburst in the car that left me reeling and knowing that I must leave immediately. Nothing was going to change unless one or both of us decided to change. Finally, I could see that all the promises of change were lies and I would no longer be sucked in and held hostage by the deception.

The strong, yet stubborn, independent woman who thought she was invincible recognized and desired change. For the sake of my kids and my life, I needed to get out and it needed to be right now. Once we safely arrived back home, in dire need for help, I called my parents. The control I once thought I possessed over my life was gone.

Finally, after sixteen years, I was ready to make a change even if he was not. My boys deserved better, I deserved better and I could not make it another day without Jesus Christ being my all. If that meant giving up the prestige I had along with the material things, I was ready. I just wanted, I needed OUT!

When my parents arrived, I was walking around like a zombie. My world was crashing down all around me. My mom promptly started to break down my household items, packing everything that was dear to us. She understood that I was on the verge of a breakdown, so she insisted that I rest while she worked. The girl who at one time made all the decisions for her family and had been in complete control was now completely helpless.

The decision to ask for and receive help was not just for me but it was for my boys too. Somehow we had protected them from a lot of the chaos and drama that was known as their life. They were out playing with friends without any knowledge or understanding of what was truly happening at home. Their entire world was changing.

Before I could put my home on the market, it was sold. Miraculously, God did in ten days what can take some many years to do, sell their homes. Seeing God move so quickly let me know I was doing the right thing. Within seventy-two hours, my entire life was in moving trucks headed to Atlanta, Georgia. In hopes of starting a new and better life, I turned my business over to my partner and my journey to restoration was in full effect.

Shake off rejection and realize it's

for your protection.

Get up and help God help you!

four

Sometimes the Bottom is the Only Way Up

My Rock Bottoms Up

The path towards healing and restoration led me straight to the home of my awesome mom and dad in Fayetteville, Georgia. After several years of international ministry travel, they were living and pastoring a church there. They had officially become "empty nesters." It had been exactly one year since they had moved into their new downsized home when my boys and I crashed their party. Blessed to have them, they provided us a safe place for healing.

When I realized the size of the little town my parents now lived in, I thought, "God, you must be punking me!

What? Why? Where in the world...?" It is this sleepy little suburban community that wraps around a town square. Nothing was happening here. There was no night life and I had always lived near the action. I did not understand why God sent me here, but it was truly the perfect place to detox from my previous life, become a normal mom and a single parent raising two boys.

Thankfully, I never completely experienced all the hardships of being a single mom. My family was an awesome support system during the time of transition. They helped me get the boys off to school and made sure they had a safe place to come home to in the afternoons. My mom, being the nurturer she is, provided exactly what we needed in that season. She and my dad loved us back to life.

My parents encouraged my immediate involvement in church. I joined the worship team but continued in the riotous lifestyle I had grown accustomed. Even though I had changed my environment, I had not allowed change to happen in my heart. Therefore, I was still the same person, just in a different location. No matter the circumstances on Saturday night, my dad would let me know that I was going to praise my way through on Sunday morning.

One Saturday night I had gone out with friends from work. I came home drunk and tried to quickly and quietly get to my bedroom. Lying there on my bed, my dad walked into my room and looked me in the eyes. He lovingly said to me, "I hope your hangover isn't too bad because in the morning you are going to praise your way through this challenge." I was startled, humbled and broken! I surely wasn't worthy to be leading anything at that time. I was having a hard time leading myself.

Everyone knows I am a daddy's girl. His love and approval are very important to me. When my dad looked me in the eyes, I was so ashamed. His reaction to me that Saturday night helped me realize that I was still heading on a collision course and change was what I so desperately needed. Never again did I desire to party and I definitely did not come home drunk again.

That moment was vital in my process of deliverance. On that Saturday night, I experienced the love and grace of my Spiritual Father through the eyes of my natural father. How easy could it have been for my dad to say, "You need to stay home tomorrow and think about what you are going to do with your life." Instead he showed me the unconditional love of God by allowing me the opportunity to still serve and lead worship.

Being allowed to remain on the worship team gave me the opportunity to continue in what I loved to do and what I was anointed to do. It also put me in position to continue in the process of deliverance. So many times when people mess up, pastors are quick to put them in a corner or on the back row casting shame upon them. Instead, my dad did exactly what Jesus would do. He showed me grace and loving kindness right in the midst of my mess. For the first time I truly understood the message of grace.

Some might call Georgia my wilderness. Nine years later, completely healed, I call it my altar. It was the place where my worship became acceptable and I learned how to be broken before God. My parents did not take me through my healing process. Yes, they covered me in prayer but they realized that what had to happen would take a one-on-one encounter between God and me. Just as Jacob told the angel that he wrestled with, "I can't let you go until you bless me," I could not rush through this process. It was to happen right here but on God's terms!

Divorce is not just real... it's painful!

My religious upbringing restricted divorce and frowned upon those who ever did such. From personal experience, I know that divorce has lifetime ramifications for the entire family. Divorce may not be your only option, but for some it might be the best option. Every marriage is different because the people are. Therefore, seek wise counsel before making the final decision to divorce.

Although divorcing was my choice, I do not condone divorce. Do whatever possible to make your marriage work. However, I had great peace in my decision to divorce. When I left the marriage, I had truly and honestly tried everything to make it work. Many times I had compromised my integrity, my children and my life. My marriage or the end of it was what brought me to my knees.

In telling my story, I have chosen to refrain from using names of my ex-husbands or anyone connected with my story other than my boys. Mom and Dad supported me in the decision to divorce because they had walked this tumultuous journey with me. They knew it was time for me to leave the marriage and live, not just for my boys and me, but for God and for YOU! Now I understand that you needed me to live through the pain and disease of my life so that you would have a tangible example of life after death. You needed to see someone rise from the ashes and live their life with purpose and passion.

The pain of divorce is real and devastating to all parties involved. It injured me, my kids and affected all my relationships. We walked through hell, but together we conquered. My ex-husband and I were both contributors to the demise of the marriage. I was broken, he was broken and together we were a broken disaster.

I got married to stay with that man for the rest of my life. I wanted the fairy tale life and to live happily ever after. No bride gets married to get divorced. No bride walks down the aisle on her wedding day singing, "I'm gonna get divorced. I'm gonna get divorced. I love my dress so much that I'm gonna wear it five more times."

Allow me to place a disclaimer here, I am by no means an advocate for divorce, but sometimes circumstances force you to do so. Of course the Bible says that in the case of adultery you are free to divorce. Nonetheless, when you are in the fight for your life and the safety of your children is compromised, it is time to GET OUT, fast! Thank God that I had a strong support system in my family to help my boys and me get through this most devastating time. Sometimes, the best thing that can happen to a relationship, even a marriage, is THE END.

The Long Way Back

Broken! That is the one word to describe me after my divorce. I was at my lowest point and mad at God for the storms I had created. It felt like my life was over and I had let everyone in my world down, my kids, my family and myself.

Driving in the darkness, looking in my rearview window at the U-hauls with our belongings, I was wondering how we would survive this. I had totally and completely hit rock bottom. Seeing the last sixteen years of our lives shoved into boxes reminded me of the failure my life had become.

However, my parents never made me feel the weight of the burden I carried. They simply embraced our downsized family and allowed us to take over their world. I would often hear them on the phone making arrangements and taking care of my personal business because I was not in the mental state to do so. At such an overwhelming time they were our backbone and personal survival kit. Often I sit and reflect, thinking, "Wow! God gave me the best parents and my kids the best Mimi and Papa on the planet."

My heart was empty and my body was completely numb. Truthfully, I thought I would never recover from this tragedy. The pain I constantly felt was not just mine, but those two precious boys of mine were hurting as well. My heart was twice broken, for me and for them. They never asked to be subjected to such dysfunctional parenting.

Change was here and a new life was on the horizon. My boys needed this stability and I needed to get healed. My recognition of the need for healing was pivotal in my deliverance. Where and how would I even begin this grueling process?

Pray, but would God really care? Was He ready to listen to all my junk? After sixteen years, I had a lot of "Junk in my trunk!" Not to mention the mess from my childhood that had fully matured. After I came through my healing process, I was able to preach a word of deliverance about "Junk in the Trunk!"

My emotions were all over the place and the devil had a grasp on my mind. He said things like, "God doesn't care about the problems you created, and you've got to live as damaged goods forever." For a while, I totally believed those words. I was damaged goods. Twice divorced, single mom and living with my parents.

AFTER SIXTEEN YEARS, I HAD A LOT OF "JUNK IN MY TRUNK!"

Remember, the enemy will always try to control your mind forcing you to live a life of oppression and depression. He will cause you to rehearse those memories of hurt, shame, anger and defeat. You will want to give up. You will feel like a turtle stuck in peanut butter not able to move forward. I want you to know that you have the same power living on the inside of you that raised Jesus from the dead. You can get up and live again. Shake, rattle and roll! Jesus has come that you might have life and that more abundantly.

> The thief does not come except to steal, and
> to kill, and to destroy. I have come that they
> may have life, and that they may have it
> more abundantly. (John 10:10)

We had been so caught up living in the now that we had made no preparations for our future. Being the ultra-independent young woman, I thought I would always make life happen. When I left home at the age of eighteen, my plans were to never return except for holidays and vacations. Yet here I was with my two boys back in my family's home.

My decline was drastic. The master closet in my 5,000 square foot home was larger than my present 10x10 bedroom in my parent's home. From a business owner with a six figure income to a $9.50 an hour job at a local department store. How was I going to support my family with this income? But God!

When you are walking in His divine will for your life, it just

YOU WILL FEEL LIKE A TURTLE STUCK IN PEANUT BUTTER, NOT ABLE TO MOVE FORWARD.

works! The redirection of my life at that point was truly a God thing. The path I had chosen was filled with destructive behaviors and bad choices. I had walked far enough and long enough according to my own way of thinking and doing. Allowing God to do the work was now my only option. Change was coming and I had to tighten up my boot straps and pull up my big girl panties to get through the mess I had created.

The enemy will attempt to paralyze us from praying and seeking God for these painful situations in our lives. What I had to do was just put one foot in front of the other and begin to move forward. Shake off rejection and realize it was for my protection. Then I had to get up and help God help me.

The story of Jonah is a great example of purposeful and divine redirection for me. Jonah was instructed by God to go to Nineveh to deliver a message of judgment. He instead attempted to escape to Tarshish aboard a ship. He knew God was merciful and would forgive the people if they repented. Why should he waste his time delivering them a judgment message when he knew God's grace?

I HAD TO PICK UP MY BOOT STRAPS AND PULL UP MY BIG GIRL PANTIES.

While on the ship, a storm arose and the sailors, trying to figure the cause, cast lots to determine who was responsible for this disaster. The lot fell on Jonah and he instructed the sailors to throw him overboard so the sea would be calm. God sends a big fish which swallows Jonah and becomes his transportation back to God's will. After three days in the belly of that big fish, Jonah lands on dry land and immediately heads to Nineveh to fulfill his purpose. Just like Jonah, I ran from my purpose of helping to pull others out of hell.

For so many years I tried hiding my pain with poor decision making and toxic relationships. Every Thursday was girl's night. When we would go out, I would always be the one dancing on the bar. "Whoop, Whoop!" The club owners would be begging my friends to get me down and take me home. I realized my friends were prophesying into my future. We had all become enablers! What I needed was to be redirected. The elimination of friendships, taking a three year sabbatical from relationships and getting lost in the presence of God was my ways of helping God help me.

Remember the man with the withered hand? Just as he had a divine encounter with Jesus so did I. It totally transformed his life and my life. This appointment changed my way of doing things. You, just like me, need to have an encounter with the love of God. He is waiting for you to allow Him to remove every defect and dysfunction in your life.

"Casting all your cares upon us for He cares
for you" (1 Peter 5:7).

What an amazing truth and promise for you my awesome friend. All you have to do is give your problems over to Him and watch God fix it for you. He is faithful, just and willing to bear your burdens. I am so thankful He is not a respecter of persons and shows no partiality. If He did it for me, He will do it for you.

It is so much easier allowing Him to direct my steps rather than continuing to make my own path. The only way you can know God's plan for your life is to spend time in His presence. His promise is that we can find Him if we search for Him.

For I know the thoughts that I think toward
you, says the LORD, thoughts of peace and
not of evil, to give you a future and a hope.
Then you will call upon Me and go and pray
to Me, and I will listen to you. And you will
seek Me and find Me, when you search for
me with all your heart. (Jeremiah 29:11-13)

Everybody wants to be a diamond,

but nobody wants to get cut!

five

When God Sets You Free, You are Truly Free Indeed

My Journey of Healing

Heartbreak is no joke! It is a sickness and my symptom was excruciating pain throughout my body. There is no prescription to expel this pain that is so real, almost tangible. Even the joints of my fingers ached and felt like they were on fire. I had never known that was even possible.

The pain had become as natural to my being as breathing. You don't really think about breathing. It is a normal occurrence unless you are congested and then every breath becomes a struggle. It is when you struggle to breathe that you appreciate each breath.

This was where I stood at that moment. I wanted to be free and I needed to be made whole. God is a gentleman, He will not go anywhere He isn't invited first and will not remove anything that has not been given to Him.

For so many years I had put all of my trust and faith in a man instead of the Man, Jesus. Well, no longer. Sick of tear stained pillows, tired of feeling worthless, broken and exposing my family to my constant erratic emotions, I just wanted to be whole and normal. I needed my kids to see me as their mom and not in a state of constant fragility. So I begged God to heal me and take the pain away, not realizing at that time how important my tears were to God.

> You number my wanderings; Put my tears
> into Your bottle;*Are they* not in Your book?
> (Psalm 6:8)

My deliverance came one night as I was lying in my bed watching a pastor on television. He was discussing the power of forgiveness and asking God to reveal the hidden places in individuals watching that evening. He was speaking to those who were allowing hurts and hang-ups to take them down a long road of unforgiveness.

He said the hidden places can be anything that you have held onto in your life and left you now merely existing. These things can hold you hostage in your life. The hidden places are buried so deep that no one, not even you know they are there. These can be triggered by a memory or possibly a scent. Hidden places can include past pains, rejection and unforgiveness. Of course I dealt with all of these, but the greatest stronghold was unforgiveness.

Before viewing this program, I thought I had already forgiven everyone. Desperate to be free from the feelings of brokenness and depression, I humbly began taking the pastor's advice. I was saying what he instructed us to say and declaring my freedom from those who had held me bound for so long.

All kinds of crazy emotions started to overwhelm my body and before long I was in the fetal position. It was then I heard the voice of the Father for the first time. He spoke gently and clearly to me, just as if He were sitting right beside me in that fetal position. He said, "Kimberly, I can't take your pain away. You will have to give it to me."

In that moment, I understood that the pain was only going to leave me when I decided to get up and walk away. The people who had labeled, rejected, used and abandoned me, I had to release them. My ex-husbands, teachers and the church people who had hurt my parents and me, I had to forgive them.

On that night I began to talk to God and give Him permission to heal me and help me walk through true forgiveness. For me, leaving that room without my healing was no longer an option. I told God, "I'm not leaving this room until You completely heal me. I don't want to feel this mess, this darkness another day of my life. P.S. My boys get up in eight hours for school so I'm going to need You to hurry!"

The 10x10 room to which I had been exiled became my place of transformation. My purpose was being birthed in that room and I completely surrendered everything to Him. All of the anger from my childhood, the resentment towards teachers who had labeled me as being learning disabled. Every single person that hurt me I removed from my VIP section and escorted them to the balcony.

I FORGIVE YOU, I RELEASE YOU

When the healing started to happen, I just let the hurt go and allowed God to do the work inside of me. He began revealing the names of people from my childhood who had hurt me. It took me literally calling their names and saying, "I FORGIVE YOU, I RELEASE YOU!"

There was a heaviness that was taken from me. I had never been able to release any of the things I had experienced to any other person, but God. He was there willing to carry me through the most difficult time of my life. For the first time, I knew God was real and my happiness was His priority. No one had ever given me the attention to detail as God had that night. I was taught by my mom and dad to read, pray and worship with them, but God gave me something that would be with me personally, always, and that was His undivided attention. For that I am forever grateful.

For the first time, God and I were experiencing such an amazing connection. Our relationship had been surface only until that night. This person who always controlled everything and never relied upon anyone had given God permission to take absolute control. Trusting God became so easy and natural after that night.

While walking through this process of healing and forgiveness, I had a visitation from God. I could see myself rocking back and forth, holding my legs close to me as though I were protecting myself. I saw bubble letters floating through the air. The words learning disability and the names of people who had crushed me filled these bubbles. Suddenly they all just floated away. God had literally kissed my pain away.

God then showed me a vision of a lady standing over a city skyline which resembled New York City. That lady was dressed in a black lacquer cat suit with a blond bouffant hairdo and bright heavy makeup. Frightfully, I recognized it was me. It was a disconcerting sight. Standing with my hands on my hips, every time I picked up my feet and walked, I would crush everything in my path without any remorse. It reminded me of the movie, "Godzilla," and the devastating effect that monster had on the city. Without any conscience, I was destroying everything under my feet.

GOD BROKE MY SPIRIT TO SAVE MY SOUL.

Also in the vision, God show me that I had the power to ruin everyone and everything in my life—and was going to—if I had not decided to submit my will and life to God. He showed me how the spirit of control is manipulated by the devil to destroy everything in our lives. Essentially, I was watching myself get delivered from ME! Those learning disability classes, that religion, the heartbreak and rejection all humbled me because of the power that God had placed in me.

I was thankful that God broke my spirit to save my soul that night. God stripped me of controlling spirits, hatred, resentment, bitterness, rejection and all of my pain. I decided that I could not change my past but I sure could help God write my future, and it was going to shine bright like a diamond. Everybody wants to be a diamond but nobody wants to get cut.

Going through the refiner's fire is not easy so many will abort the mission of healing too quickly. Oh no, not me, I was determined to no longer live in defeat. I am thankful I stayed there in that small room until God completed His work inside of me. Prior to this, I had spent many nights crying so hard, lying awake thinking about all the "what if's" and "maybe if's."

All the things I had held so close such as hurt, betrayal and embarrassment now made sense to me and that every ounce of pain I had experienced was for a reason. I no longer hated those memories nor regretted those seasons. God showed me that He was working all things for my good.

That night I spent more time with God than ever before. I had traveled the world with many well-known pastors and evangelists, singing on their praise and worship teams. For many years I sang about His presence but, I had never spent time there until that night. Now everything I had sung about and heard my daddy preach about was real to me. Nothing in the world could compare to what I felt that night. It was the ultimate experience. And because of God's omnipresence, I now have permanent access to Him daily, anywhere or at any time. I always did.

As I sat in my room just basking in the ambience of His glory I began to sing. For the first time it wasn't just something I did because I could, it was from a place of reverential worship. There was a worshiper living on the inside of me and she was now screaming to get out.

As a child, I had decided singing was all I could do because my daddy did not believe in women preachers. There were times I resented my ability to sing when my heart's desire was to preach. However, on this night of deliverance, singing was just what I needed. The sound of my worship freed my soul. Just as I sat there in my room, the words began to flow from my spirit about His majesty, His greatness.

This was just the start of what God was going to do in and through my life. The healing process was not going to be an easy one, but handing it over to Him was exactly what I needed to do. I wanted to be free from the condemnation of my past.

We are all human and make mistakes, but God has the last word. He can take those with the worst past and give them the very best future. I was broken from the inside out, 'tore up from the floor up', but look at me now. The enemy is defeated and I am more than a conqueror.

Totally and completely broken before Him, I determined to never go back to my old way of living. I wanted to stay there in His presence forever. For the first time I put a demand on God for my soul and He showed out! In just eight hours God had completely set me free from my past to set me up for the start of my new future in Him. As I began my new life, I saw the world differently and my ears were completely opened to hearing His voice. I began to understand the mind of Christ!

> For who has known the mind of the Lord
> that he may instruct him? But we have the
> mind of Christ. (I Corinthians 2:16)

There is a scripture that I quote to myself so often and it helps to keep me on track for God's will in my life.

> For in Him we live and move and have our
> being, as also some of your own poets have
> said, 'For we are also His
> offspring.'
> (Acts 17:28)

Is it easy to lose focus? Yes, of course. To stay on track you cannot allow the cares of life to overwhelm you. The more I

HE CAN TAKE THOSE WITH THE WORST PAST AND GIVE THEM THE VERY BEST FUTURE.

get into God's word and understand that I can't work enough, pray enough, or preach hard enough to earn His grace, an overwhelming peace revitalizes my spirit. I realize that Jesus went to the cross for my sins and I am living in Him! You have that same promise because my God is an impartial God and does not show favoritism to any gender, class, culture or color! If He set me free, He will do the same for you!

Part 2

my present

Christians are like glow sticks, they must be broken in order to shine.

six

Wholeness Births Peace and Success in God

My Healing

There was purpose in my pain. The rejection I had felt for so long wasn't someone necessarily wanting me out of their lives but someone God needed out of my future. Where God has ordained for you to go, everyone is not invited. The people who have hurt, betrayed and left you were not meant to be in your future. The curtain had closed on my sixteen year marriage but that did not mean the production was over. There was still so much to live for and I was to be the star of my comeback story.

My two precious sons were depending on me to be the woman God had already written about in His Book before I was ever in my mother's womb. The very best of my days were in the rest of my days. You see, He knew what I would become, even while I was living in darkness, not knowing how I would turn my life around.

> Your eyes saw my substance, being yet unformed. And in Your book they all were written, The days fashioned for me, When as yet there were none of them. (Psalm 139:16)

So many of my friends and family were no longer in my life at this time and the enemy had convinced me that I would always be this way, alone and bitter. But God! In His Word, He promises never to leave or forsake me.

> Be strong and of good courage, do not fear nor be afraid of them; for the LORD your God, He is the One who goes with you. He will not leave you nor forsake you."
> (Deuteronomy 31:6)

Through the years I had hardened my heart so that no one in my life could ever hurt me again. On the inside, I was still that little girl who had been labeled learning disabled and I was determined that I could and would protect myself. In doing so, I was trying to take God's place in my life. It was such a great feeling to finally relinquish the control of my life over to Him. So many people want to be healed and walk in forgiveness but they do not understand the process.

In my decision to get better and not to remain bitter, I said to God, "I don't want to be mean, hard, and sad another day of my life. Please help me!" When God and I shifted shoulders, He took those burdens and I felt an unforgettable peace. No longer were the words of other people controlling me. No longer was I controlled by my pain or emotion. The best way to enjoy the promised abundant life is to be totally and completely set free from people and their opinions. Experiencing His freedom was the greatest feeling ever. Truly broken before Him, I became real with myself and with God. From personal testimony I know, "Whom the Son sets free is free indeed!"

Therefore if the Son makes you free, you
shall be free indeed. (John 8:36)

Christians are like glow sticks, they must be broken in order to shine. Completely broken from my marriage, the divorce and the judgment of other people, my worship became just like that of the woman in Luke chapter seven. Her life was far less than perfect and she was constantly judged by everyone in her life. This did not stop her from coming to Jesus.

She had heard about this man who loved others unconditionally but today she was going to experience it. Knowing that her box of ointment was her most precious possession, it was said to have been a year's worth of wages, she was giving her all that day. She broke her alabaster box filled with precious ointment anointing the feet of Jesus and drying them with her hair. Just as this woman, here I was, sobbing and pouring out my tears before God. He received our worship because beautifully broken is where God does His best work.

Please do not think my deliverance was easy or it was over in one night. I had to get up, move forward and live outside of that room. Although I had been delivered from people, I had to remember, those same people had not been delivered. Miracles are easy to get but hard to keep and in my opinion so is deliverance. You can be rescued from your past in a moment. However, you must continually walk in that freedom every day of your life and in every area of your life!

For me, it took time and commitment to the process. Every day I made the decision to wake up and get out of bed, get dressed and put one foot in front of the other. This was just a part of my journey to maintain my healing. Remember, God is a gentleman and He is waiting on you to approach His throne daily! Forgiveness and freedom are yours! It is up to you to act upon that promise today and go get it!

During this time, my dad told me about a painful experience setting the stage for grace in his life. There was an unforgettable time in his teen years when he was molested by his dad's friend. My dad was devastated and knew he could never tell anyone because this vibrant, handsome, popular man was loved by everyone.

In those days, no one spoke about molestation. He carried this horrible secret until after he was married to my mom. He then forgave that man, not because he deserved it or even desired it, but because it would set my dad free to pursue his purpose from God.

After learning this, my admiration for my dad increased. He did not allow the sins of another destroy the purpose and plan of God for his life. Amazingly, my dad was a normal man, great husband and loving father. No one would ever have known that he had this secret locked up in a corner of his heart.

God had taken the most horrific encounter and helped my dad to become a great man of faith and grace. He truly knew how to let those hurts go and allow healing to manifest not only in his personal life but his spiritual life as well. God did not cause this grievance to afflict him but God used his pain to give him empathy for those who have been affected by molestation.

Through personal experience and now the testimony of my dad, I have seen God use past mistakes and storms to transform and save the lives of others from the same or similar disastrous paths. If you are willing to open your heart, accept healing and avail to him, your mess will become your message and your pain will become your purpose.

Toxic Soul Ties

Still needing to get rid of the things or people that continued to contaminate my life and my worship, I asked God to reveal and heal more of the hidden places. Many times you will feel as though you are totally whole and yet there can be lingering influences that can steal your focus and cause you to lose the joy and power given to you by God. He revealed things that had kept me bound and repeating cycles. I just wanted to pass the test! I knew that if I did not pass this test, I would be struggling with the same or similar situations in the future.

Before, during and after my marriage, I have been in some very toxic relationships. After much reading and research, I discovered and learned everything I could about soul ties that are birthed out of toxic relationships. There are two types of soul ties, healthy and unhealthy. Ungodly relationships form unhealthy soul ties while Godly relationships form healthy soul ties. The healthy soul ties build us up, provide wisdom and give Godly counsel. Unhealthy soul ties are ungodly relationships that have become toxic.

God wants us to have healthy, meaningful relationships. Well, I had the opposite. They developed through friendships, vows, commitments, and physical intimacy. Other examples of ungodly relationships that form unhealthy soul ties include:

- Abusive and controlling relationships (physically, sexually, emotionally, verbally)
- Adulterous affairs
- Sex before marriage

In my prayer time, first I asked God to help me break all the unhealthy soul ties. Then, I asked him to replace them with Godly people that would influence me to become the woman He had purposed me to be. Strategically, God brought in the right people and I started to form those Godly relationships and healthy soul ties. He started changing my thinking and I became filled with joy unspeakable.

In Deuteronomy 1:2, we read about the children of Israel who were on an eleven day journey to Canaan. Because they were stubborn, disobedient, rebellious, and unfaithful complainers, they wandered around in the wilderness for forty years. After the first generation died, it had to be their decision to quit grumbling, complaining and rebelling against God for Him to move them into their purpose and promise land. Finally, I got it! God would change my life when I became workable!

The best remedy for heartbreak is making the decision to get healed and knowing you are worth the investment. For so long I did not feel worthy of love or even God's forgiveness. So beaten down and battered, I honestly thought God was so very mean. As a child, I would hear my mom praying and she would become so emotional. For an answered prayer, I thought you had to beg God. Listening to her, I would think, "God, You are mean. Why does my mom have to cry like that to get a prayer through?" Later, I learned it was just my mom's passion for the Lord of her life, Jesus Christ, and the spirit of intercession. Worship is personal and everyone worships in his or her own way.

When I am ministering and preaching about the love of God, it is no longer about me and my ability to change lives but instead, it is about fulfilling God's will in my life and watching Him transform others. One of my most precious times is seeing the countenance of people change in the presence of God. It is in His presence all brokenness is revealed and the beginning of their journey to restoration. Tears are flowing down their cheeks. Some, for the first time, are allowed to be vulnerable. All of their past hurts, current habits and future hang-ups are being exposed to the Savior and inner healing is taking place.

On the outside many people will appear as though their life is perfect, never willing to expose their pains. My life, marriage and entrepreneurial success were great examples of living a life of delusion. During the day, I was building relationships with powerful people who were beautiful on the outside but totally broken on the inside. Familiar with the need to camouflage my brokenness and pretending I had it all together, their pain was easy to recognize. To the world, everything on the outside appeared to be great, but don't you dare look on the inside. Attempting to take away the pain, I would drink my way into oblivion, falling into a restless sleep only to awaken the next morning to face life's hardships. I was wondering how I would make it through one more day.

After many years of self-induced flu or hangover, I am so thankful to have met my "rock bottom!" A place where I comprehended the love of God and knew I could not go on without Him being the center of my world! At that place is where I discovered myself as God sees me with a worshipper's heart as well as a powerful call to ministry. Starting to really understand the unconditional love and embracing His forgiveness for myself, I discovered my "sweet soft side", learned to trust God and released forgiveness to others.

If I had not allowed God to "break my spirit to save my soul," I would not be who I am today. My God loves us too much to leave us the way we are; dejected, embittered, and in misery. Sometimes He lets your stubborn self walk into a storm head on (you know, the one you created) so that you'll hit rock bottom and change your perspective of Him and see the life He has planned for you.

God has a plan to bless us and not to harm us. He is not a respecter of persons. No matter where or who we are, He has got us! All He is wanting is total surrender. Now, put one step in front of the other and start walking out your deliverance. Pray for specifics! I did it and so can you. Make the decision today! No more settling for less than God's best for your life. He has come that we may have life and have it more abundantly.

The thief does not come except to steal, and
to kill, and to destroy. I have come that they

may have life, and that they may have it
more abundantly. (John 10:10)

There was nothing like hitting rock bottom to make me grateful for everything I have in my life and discovering something new. It was not until I reached that point of total surrender that I turned my face completely toward God, acknowledged my sin and the inability to handle my life. In this vulnerable position, I was praying and crying out to God to destroy the lifetime of pain and unforgiveness and asking Him to rescue me from total destruction and begin to mend my heart. He broke every chain and stronghold that had held me captive for so long! HE DID IT ALL! He will do the same for you, I am absolutely confident. He does not want anyone to be destroyed, but wants everyone to repent and live their best life.

The Lord is not slack concerning His
promise, as some count slackness, but is
longsuffering toward us, not willing that any
should perish but that all should come to
repentance. (2 Peter 3:9)

Only God truly knows our hearts and, when we sincerely want Him to change our situation, He will.

Then, and only then, will He completely enter our hearts. Paul explains and defines true repentance and godly sorrow.

"For godly sorrow produces repentance
leading to salvation, not `to be regretted; but
the sorrow of the world produces death."
(II Corinthians 7:10)

OUR MESS BECOMES OUR MESSAGE AND OUR PAIN BECOMES OUR PURPOSE.

God will use our sorrow to capture our undivided attention. True repentance produces immediate transformation. With my acceptance, the Holy Spirit changed my life, my focus, and my view of the world. I no longer needed to pretend to have a successful marriage or a perfect life. God was going to use me just as I was, broken before Him.

Seeking God's true purpose for my life, I was now presenting my body as a living sacrifice. I wanted to be HOLY and ACCEPTABLE unto God. This, as Romans 12:1 states, "is my reasonable service," or the least I could do to honor all He had done for me. My desire was to be pleasing in His sight.

> And whatever we ask we receive from Him,
> because we keep His commandments and do
> those things that are pleasing in His sight.
> (1 John 3:22)

Learning to put my FAITH in God and no longer in man, I began to have confidence in the Bible and reading with purpose. Desperately needing to understand all of God's promises for my life, I was meditating on and hiding His word in my heart both day and night. Downloading them into my spirit, I became hungry to know more so I would read books about healing. You become what you meditate on and if your mind is on trivial things in life, you will be become frivolous.

> Your word I have hidden in my heart, that I
> might not sin against You. (Psalms 119:11)

Most importantly, I got involved in my family's church where I was shown unconditional love. It was there I learned the concept of "loving people back to life." I wanted to express that same kind of love to those who were broken in my life.

Born a worshipper and in the fire of revival with my family, I could never live in the smoke of traditionalism and, every time I entered into worship, I was realizing my purpose. As He was healing me, all other things I desired (according to His will) would come in due season.

> And let us not grow weary while doing good,
> for in due season we shall reap if we do not
> lose heart. (Galatians 6:9)

To tell you that I am excited about my life and future in Christ Jesus is an understatement! Daily I am amazed at how God works through situations and answers my prayers!

> But as it is written: "Eye has not seen, nor
> ear heard, Nor have entered into the heart of
> man the things which God has prepared for
> those who love Him."(1 Corinthians 2:9)

Through my broken mess and
brokenness, God turned my scars
into stars, my mess into my message
and my pain into my pulpit.

seven

Conquering Hell in High Heels

My Ministry

Wholeness is brokenness. Repeat those words aloud! Saying them makes more sense than actually just reading or hearing them said to you. In my time of healing and transformation, I learned to remain broken before Him. The work He was doing in me would not be a onetime occurrence; it was a lifetime journey toward perfection. Perfection, not as we think in the natural, but spiritual maturity.

Through my broken mess and brokenness, God turned my scars into stars, my mess into my message and my pain into my pulpit. I learned you cannot fix spiritual problems with natural solutions. If I remain broken it allows God to enter in and make full use of every part of me.

My experience with religion had been one of hardened people who had built walls to surround them. They allowed no one in and nothing out. Therefore, the true blessings and benefits of living in Christ could not penetrate their spirit or infiltrate their life.

These kinds of people are very easy to discover. They have a critical spirit, always seeing the negative, never expecting the positive. In my opinion, the worst thing is to know the word of God but not *knowing* the work of God. This sounds like a play on words, however when you truly know the word of God and allow it to penetrate your spirit, it will change you daily. So many have a head knowledge with no heart knowledge. There is a difference in knowing the Bible and knowing the author. In knowing the author, I learn the Word and can rightly divide its truths in my life and in the lives of those around me.

"Religiatards" is the term I use to describe those religious and critical people who have head knowledge but no actual faith. They can quote every scripture that will benefit them in being critical and judgmental but do not understand the humility that Jesus portrayed and the grace displayed as He walked the earth. It amazes me how Jesus just loved people so much that

He even took their sins in His body to the cross to make them righteous.

> Who Himself bore our sins in His own body
> on the tree, that we, having died to sins,
> might live for righteousness—by whose
> stripes you were healed. (I Peter 2:24)

When I was divorcing my husband, what I did not need was sermons or lectures on divorce. I did not need to be kicked when I was already down. No one goes to their wedding thinking divorce. They truly believe this is until death do us part and I am going to stay with this person for the rest of my life, bad breath and all. The Bible says, "When you see your brother in a ditch, help him out."

For if they fall, one will lift up his companion. But woe to him who is alone when he falls, For he has no one to help him up. (Ecclesiastes 4:10)

So many Christians would rather grab a shovel and help bury you than help. While others will just walk right by and gossip about you to others, God has created me to be a heart healer. I was once described by a friend to her congregation as, "not your mom's preacher." I truly felt that to be a genuine compliment to the type of ministry God has called me to do.

My purpose in God is to take these people who have been battered, abused and left for dead and love them back to life. Some people have been cheated on by their spouses, while others have been molested by their daddies and so many abandoned by their parents. Some hurts are more intense than others and all carry a large burden of seeking to forgive the oppressor. These are the precious people God has trusted me to love back to life.

In my deliverance, I learned that loving people was so critical because I was given the responsibility to love the hardest people. In my old life, I did not even like people, so loving them was not even possible. But God turned that around and gave me an insatiable love for His people. Most of the people I encounter are so hardened by life and its complications. They have erected a wall of defense to protect their broken hearts. God has anointed me to speak and at the sound of my voice, the walls begin to crumble.

So many women and men testify of what God has done through me. I receive text messages, inboxes and calls almost daily about how their lives were forever changed after hearing me preach or following me on social media. I am amazed that as people encounter the healing anointing of the Holy Spirit and tears begin to flow, they are delivered from years of abuse that has almost crippled their very existence.

It is for them that I must remain broken before God. In my time of healing, I availed myself to God. I gave Him total access to my pain and the liberty to allow me to feel the pain. I had lived years just existing and not living in my personal life. I had created such a strong wall of defense that I was almost impenetrable until I had that one-on-one encounter with God. It had been so long since I had truly known peace. I had been so hard hearted trying to protect me, but I knew I wanted to feel again.

The pain I was enduring I definitely did not enjoy, however I understood the necessity. I kept reminding myself that I had asked God to allow me to feel again. Whatever that looked like, I just wanted to have that heart of flesh and experience true love in my personal life. The Bible tells us to pick up our cross daily. Until you submit to the will of God for your life, your cross will be really tough to bear. It becomes easier to carry your cross when you realize the reason for the load.

Healed people heal people

God was giving me a unique gift of healing. Instead of the laying on of hands, we hug it out until the healing is real, tangible and visible. 'Hugs melt the pain away' is what I believe. To remain effective in my gifting, it is imperative that I continue to be broken before God. That does not mean I am broken as I was before, but I am spiritually broken. Broken for a purpose! I cannot allow myself to falter and go back to the old way of life. I have to remain in a constant place of availability to God. My desire is for Him to get the glory out of my life. For this to happen I must constantly present myself to Him. Just because I am delivered does not mean I don't face challenges. However, if I approach God in humility He will help me overcome my struggles.

The LORD is close to the brokenhearted
and saves those who are crushed in spirit.
(Psalms 34:18)

The pivotal moment in my time of healing came Mother's Day 2009. MySpace featured a test on its site, "Twenty-Five Random Things About Me." It was a very simple game or questionnaire that had gone viral. I remember thinking and saying to myself, "I really don't know me. I don't know my favorite color, food or hobby."

Just like the chameleon known for its quick ability to change colors to blend in or fit their environment, that was me. For the chameleon it is a protective mechanism, just like me. Whatever friend I was around, in an instant I could be just like them. Then I recognized that I was a complete mess. Sitting there in my bed I asked God to please reveal twenty-five things about me. Never could

I have imagined or dreamed that God would use my youngest son Lyncoln to fulfill my request.

It was the morning of Mother's Day when Lyncoln came into my room and brought me the most precious gift. Just thinking of it still brings me to tears. Just like most moms when their children give them a gift, no matter the reason or season, I excitedly opened the package. Lyncoln had composed the most amazing poem for me and had placed it inside the most beautiful frame.

You are beautiful, you are kind
You love me when I am annoying
You sing like an angel
You buy me things
You work hard for my needs, you provide for me
You make the world stop when you laugh
You give me hugs that make me love
you more and more each day
You don't complain when you are mad
You make people happy with your smile
You care for me, you cry with me when I am sad
You love those hated, you make the world different
You are superwoman
You somehow become friends with your enemies
You laugh at bad memories
You survived hell in high heels
You are triumphant
You yell at me with a grin

You make people feel beautiful
You make me feel very appreciative
You give me things I don't deserve
You make me laugh when you yell at me
You make other moms jealous
You don't care what other people think about you
You snuggle with me
You scream my name at basketball games
You smile like the sun, you are unlike any other
You bought me Christmas when you didn't have to
You always smell good, you don't
take crap from anyone
You laugh at mistakes, you forgive
me when I make mistakes
You give me grace, you say sorry
when you make mistakes
You love God
You laugh at my jokes even when they're not funny
You give me advice, you tell me that everything is okay
My favorite thing that I love about you is that........
You are you

-- Lyncoln Doggett

This poem will always be one of the most precious gifts received in my lifetime. Given to me at one of the lowest points of my life, it was a demonstration of God's love for me. My young son knew me better than

I knew myself. After I divorced, I felt like a total failure every time I looked in my boys' eyes. It was amazing how God used what I thought was my greatest failure to catapult me into my ministry of healing.

God uses people in our lives at strategic times to set us back on track and I totally love that about Him. If God could use my thirteen-year-old son to begin healing my broken heart, He could use me to begin the healing in you and the hearts of so many. What I find to be so amazing, I had only asked for twenty-five things about myself and God gave me thirty!

God said through the prophet Joel, "So I will restore to you the years that the swarming locusts has eaten." (Joel 2:25a) God loves to restore what has been taken in our lives. That's God's specialty.

My parents sang a song when I was a small child, "When you've tried everything and everything has failed, try Jesus." For a young woman who had grown up hearing my parents praying for and with others, watching their lifestyle of worship, and seeing their faith encouraged me to try Jesus.

Finally, I realized that God had never given up on me. My mom would always say that God was a gentleman. He was sensitive to my needs and yet He never forced His love on me. When I was ready, He was. For someone so broken and weak, God gave me strength.

I can do all things through Christ who
strengthens me. (Philippians 4:13)

I can say that I learned to never make permanent
decisions based on my temporary crisis. You see, as
long as I have a pulse God has a plan. If you don't
use your mistake to keep making mistakes, you'll get
better and not bitter. Although I am healed, I still face
challenges and storms. But I absolutely refuse to get
stuck in the storm or to be broken by them ever again.
You see, I am stronger and wiser because I know that
every storm runs out of rain.

While traveling with my parents in evangelism, we
would run into heavy rainstorms. While everyone else
was sitting on the side of the road waiting for the storm
to pass, my dad would slow the car down and keep
moving. His belief was that we would pass through the
downpour. He refused to stop and let that storm cloud
keep dumping on us. In life, we have a choice to make.
As life throws us curves, we can choose to allow life to
break us or make us.

You fall in love with their charisma
but you live with their character.

eight

Marriage God's Way

My Happily Ever After

After my divorce, dating was not an option. I had been married most of my adult life and had no desire to even look at a man. So for three years I put a "DO NOT DISTURB" sign on my heart and I became lost in the presence of God seeking out my purpose. I was determined to use the same bricks to build another house.

This was the time I needed to find myself in God and my boys needed to have their mom without interruption. Surprisingly, I enjoyed being single. But most importantly, I was finally able to be there for my boys.

During this time, so much started happening within me. First, I discovered my true purpose through prayer, fasting and reading the Word. Second, the passion to truly love people was birthed and cultivated. My hope was for every person I would encounter to desire a love relationship with Jesus Christ. Third, I learned how to become submissive. Being submitted to God first taught me why I am to walk in submission to my husband.

After three years of being single I was lying in my bed praying. It was Father's Day and I remember reading my son's blog about Father's Day being just another day. I realized then that my boys needed a man in their lives who would treat me with honor and love and show them how to treat their wives. Without thought or hesitation I said to God, "Send me a husband." I was like, "Whoa, wait. Who has just invaded my body?" I was completely happy single. Sure, sometimes I would get lonely at night, but I would just surround my body with seventeen pillows and sleep like a baby.

With great confidence I moved forward with the desire that God apparently had placed inside of me. God is omniscient; He knows what we need and when we need it. He knew it was time for my ministry to take off and I was going to need spiritual covering.

Anxiously, I began to prepare myself for our meeting. In our finite mind we think God will put that spouse right where we want to meet them. I became more cognizant of my surroundings, expecting to find this man.

However, God had other plans. He said to me, "I have a man for you but you are not ready." What? Baffled at this revelation, I began to seek God for clarity. God gently said, "It's your mouth! You have to get your mouth under control." I was still not fully comprehending what God was saying to me. All I knew was that I was preaching all over the country, leading our local worship group and encouraging men and women all over the world through my social media pages. Why would I need to get my mouth under control?

God continued to speak to me saying, "The man I have for you is so submitted to me that you would destroy him with your toxic attitude and words." God was still working on me. Even today, I still work on me daily by spending time in God's presence. You see, anything you don't deal with will follow you through your entire life. You're up one day and down the next. If you don't deal with those roots of pain, whether generational curses or sins you have created, you give Satan permission to antagonize you in these areas. God will not anoint what He did not appoint.

God began to speak clearly to me about this man He had prepared just for me. He shared private intimate moments this man was having with Him. Later I learned that every Tuesday evening he was having a date with

God. He was so lost in the presence of God that he would not look up until God had instructed Him to do so. Of course my first thought was, "Oh no, he is a religitard."

When I met Mark I was not at all interested in dating him. We were both so lost in our purpose and serving God. He and I shared a few conversations on Facebook. As a matter of fact, he was dating someone and had suggested she read my daily posts. That probably was not very smart of him but it worked out great for me. Needless to say, she took offense and their relationship was short lived thereafter.

We began an awesome friendship and then decided to exchange phone numbers. We would talk on the phone and end our conversations with prayer. One particular conversation, Mark asked me to pray. The Holy Spirit spoke to me that this man wants a praying woman and this is

GOD WILL NOT ANOINT WHAT HE DID NOT APPOINT.

a test. I thought, "Oh yeah, I've got a prayer for you." I began to pray speaking in an elevated tone as I decreed and declared a blessing over his life. I heard him (Mark) say, "Oh yeah, I'm going to marry this woman."

Mark was the greatest gift God has given to me and my boys. He showed my boys how their mother was supposed to be loved and appreciated. This man tells me about five hundred times a day, "I love you. I am so proud of you." I cannot even tell you how fulfilling it is to hear him thanking my parents continually for giving birth to me, his love.

When God brought Mark into our lives, God gave me everything I never knew I wanted but everything I needed. Both he and I will admit that neither of us would have chosen each other, but God brought us together. We are strong individuals, but a powerful force together.

I had already started my ministry when Mark and I started dating. I was just beginning to preach and finding God's will for my life. He came into my world and showed me how to study the word in-depth. He added to my ministry and never once tried to take away from what God had for me to do.

We shared the same passion for loving people. He loves God so much more than he loves me and that love spills over into our marital relationship. He gives me freedom to just be me. Because he is fifteen years older than me, Mark is very confident in himself. His desire is to take care of me and fulfill my needs.

I'm sure as you read this chapter, you either cannot believe that we could have this kind of marriage after our failures or you are wondering whether there are other men like Mark. I can only tell you what I know and that is God truly brought us together.

When I realized that broken attracts broken, I never again wanted to throw myself into any kind of relationship that wasn't totally centered on God's plan for my life. I realized I could be happy without a man in my life as I centered my focus on Jesus Christ. I now know that you must be contented in your singleness to ever become a good partner in marriage.

I had immersed myself in teaching CDs and learning to enjoy God's Word. I wanted to make sure that those negatives in my life that had almost broken me could no longer rule my present nor future. I learned that forgiveness is when you bear the pain that someone has given you but you no longer carry the burden of it.

MARK IS MY ESCAPE AND NOT MY DUTY.

God then sends me a man who has been a student of the word for thirty years. He deeply believes that you must be a student of the Bible to be able to live a strong Christian life. He has mentored me in understanding the revelations of the Scripture, and today our lives revolve around our personal worship and study time plus the time we spend together in prayer each day.

If a person is only attached to you, they will leave when better opportunities come along. There will be no loyalty in the relationship. When we said, "I do," we determined that it truly is for life. We both had lived in brokenness and were now willing for God to direct our present and future. Willingness is the key that goes into the lock and opens the door that allows God to begin to remove our character defects. We can now live knowing that openness is to wholeness as secrets are to sickness. We realize you are only as sick as your secrets. We share each other's life without judgment because we love as is directed in Ephesians 5. Mark is my escape and not my duty.

Wives, submit to your own husbands, as
to the Lord. For the husband is head of the
wife, as also Christ is head of the church;
and He is the Savior of the body. Therefore,
just as the church is subject to Christ, so
let the wives be to their own husbands in
everything. Husbands, love your wives, just
as Christ also loved the church and gave
Himself for her, that He might sanctify and
cleanse her with the washing of water by the
word, that He might present her to Himself a
glorious church, not having spot or wrinkle
or any such thing, but that she should be
holy and without blemish. So husbands
ought to love their own wives as their own
bodies; he who loves his wife loves himself.
(Ephesians 5:22-28)

You don't have to live in defeat another day. When you understand your God-ordained destiny, it assists you in determining life's purpose today, for tomorrow. As I head to the airport weekly to fly to ministries around the world, I am confident that my husband is covering me in my calling because he knows who he is in Christ.

Our lives today revolve around God's purpose. We know that you can't get breakthrough in a drive through. I have people asking me how to establish a social media ministry that will catapult them into success. I can only say that to be sold out means you cannot be bought.

God has trusted me to shepherd so many people via social media. I do not at all take that opportunity lightly. Sure, I have found success and favor with man, but this was costly. Many could not survive what I had to endure and have experienced in life. Thankfully, I survived what killed so many before and after me. There is no way for me to duplicate or teach this. You just have to live through it. I could not have known or imagined this would happen to me.

MARK AND I REALIZED THAT WE WERE ASSIGNED, NOT ATTACHED TO EACH OTHER.

When I first moved back in with my parents and got plugged into social media, I never thought I would have such a strong and immediate following of thousands. This was not my intention. I just wanted to help people. Encourage them to be better and not bitter, walk in forgiveness and love God. I had traveled the world leading praise and worship but, who knew I would again travel the world preaching in some of the greatest churches. God has connected me with people who had become so broken by life and hardened by circumstances beyond their control.

I watch people cry for the first time in years and forgive the father or mother who had wounded them. Almost weekly I walk people through the tragedy of divorce, rape, molestation and suicidal attempts. The people I pray with are fragile and need people who can be strong and intercede on their behalf. What I do is not for the income but the outcome. My husband and I believe in God and His power to heal. His love melts the pain away.

Above all, love each other deeply, because
love covers over a multitude of sins.
(1 Peter 4:8, NIV)

Love is patient, love is kind. It does not envy,
it does not boast, it is not proud.
(1 Corinthians 13:4, NIV)

Nothing can separate you from the love of God. God used situations in our lives to move us to surrender. We know that anointing will get you to your purpose but character keeps you there.

Anointing will get you to your purpose
but character keeps you there.

nine

Get Up, Get Out

Getting You Unstuck

You have read my story of restoration and healing. Now let me help you to begin your journey to freedom in Christ. If you did not accept Jesus at the beginning of this book, turn back to page xvii in the introduction and pray that prayer. Make Him the most important part of your life. Begin a love relationship with the Savior of this world.

Welcome back and congratulations on your decision to accept Jesus as your personal Savior. From this point forward your life will never ever be the same. Will there be obstacles and oppositions? Yes, but now you have the same power that raised Jesus from the dead living on the inside of you. Paul understood this message as he stated in Galatians 2:20, "I have been crucified with Christ: It is no longer I who live, but Christ lives in me; And the life which I now live in the flesh I live by faith in the Son of God, Who loved me and gave Himself for me." As a member of the family of Christ, you have been authorized to access that power to help you overcome anything that will come against you.

Now let's resume the journey. Many of you might find yourselves in situations where it seems as though there is no way out. I am here to let you know that you can be free and free indeed. So, accepting Christ is going to be crucial to your journey of total deliverance.

If the Son sets you free, you will be free
indeed (John 8:36)

It does not matter the situation you are facing. There is nothing too hard for God. There is no problem too big or small. He cares about everything you care about. God is amazing. He knows your problems before you ever present them to Him. All He is waiting for you to do is trust Him to solve the problems. The Bible is full of people who had problems. I have learned in order for there to be a miracle, there must first be a problem.

Right now get a notebook or journal and take note of the problem or problems you are facing. You have just taken the first step and admitted that you have a problem that you cannot handle or fix in your own power. You truly need the power of God. Underneath it write the words, "Lord, I am handing my problems over to you. I no longer want to live with this in my life. Today (write the date), I am shifting shoulders with you. I am exchanging my burdens for yours."

You have just given your problems to the problem solver. When you are willing to admit that you need help, you will then transfer it to God. He is faithful to step in and be that help you need. As I stated in a previous chapter, I

MIRACLES ARE EASY TO GET BUT HARD TO KEEP.

begged God to take away my pain. I then realized that I had to give it to Him. I had to give my problems away.

From Lame to Leaping

> Now Peter and John went up together to the temple at the hour of prayer, the ninth hour. And a certain man lame from his mother's womb was carried, whom they laid daily at the gate of the temple which is called Beautiful, to ask alms from those who entered the temple; who, seeing Peter and John about to go into the temple, asked for alms. And fixing his eyes on him, with John,

Peter said, "Look at us." So he gave them his attention, expecting to receive something from them. Then Peter said, "Silver and gold I do not have, but what I do have I give you: In the name of Jesus Christ of Nazareth, rise up and walk." And he took him by the right hand and lifted him up, and immediately his feet and ankle bones received strength. So he, leaping up, stood and walked and entered the temple with them—walking, leaping, and praising God. And all the people saw him walking and praising God. 10 Then they knew that it was he who sat begging alms at the Beautiful Gate of the temple; and they were filled with wonder and amazement at what had happened to him. (Acts 3:1-10)

I HAVE LEARNED THAT FOR THERE TO BE A MIRACLE, THERE MUST FIRST BE A PROBLEM.

The lame man was laid day after day at the gate called Beautiful. He was like so many of you who have been going through life only existing. Never experiencing the abundant life promised in John 10:10, which says, "I have come that they may have life, and that they may have it more abundantly." God is delivering you, so no longer accept the cardboard box people have put you in, decorating it, and calling it home. Watch out for people in your life who once carried you into your dysfunction. Those people who enable you and give you a free pass to NOT be all that God has called you to be.

Sometimes people do not want to see you healed and walking in your awesome destiny. They want you to live an ordinary life when God wants you to live an extraordinary life. Ordinary is the enemy of miracles! I believe God does exceedingly above all that we can ask or think.

> Now to Him who is able to do exceedingly
> abundantly above all that we ask or think,
> according to the power that works in us.
>
> (Ephesians 3:20)

This lame man could hear, see, think, talk but he couldn't walk. He had entered the world in this condition. His ankles lacked the strength that gave him the ability to walk as you and I, so his family and friends faithfully carried him to the gate every day. People will label you once they lay you where they think you belong just like the lame man's friends did at the gate.

What is it that makes you lame? Some of you are lame because of something that happened to you at a young age and you can't let go of it. Some of you are lame because of a divorce. You are so broken and bitter that you can't move forward. Some of you are lame because of that job that you worked at for years and you were close to your retirement, but they handed you a pink slip. Now you are so angry and you can't seem to move forward. Some of you may be lame because you are facing infertility. You have tried everything and nothing is working. Maybe you're lame because your dad walked out on your mom and your family and as a result you suffer with abandonment issues.

You need to start speaking to your situation. Wishing you could walk will not make you walk. We pray as though God doesn't know our challenges. Stop allowing your challenges to cripple you. Help God help you. Get up and get out!

Finally, after years and years of people laying him at the gate and leaving him there to beg for alms, Peter and John decided to not throw coins in his bucket but instead they took action. They commanded him to get up and walk, taking him by the hand and lifting him. We all need radical friends who will lift us out of our dysfunction.

Your deliverance can happen in three stages; the limping, the lifting and the leaping. While stages one and two can happen simultaneously, the third stage is your goal. As I have stated before, a miracle is easy to get but hard to keep, therefore you must allow yourself to go through the first two stages of deliverance.

Think of this process like a child first learning to walk. He starts with pulling up on furniture around the house. He struggles to find his balance and might fall several times maybe incurring injuries. Yet those who love him continue to encourage him to keep trying. It would be abnormal for them to continue to just carry him when he has the potential to learn to walk.

Stage One: LIMPING

The limping stage is the initiator of your deliverance. You have sought God to move on your behalf, but He is requiring *you* to move. You finally have decided enough is enough. I do not have to lie here any longer and settle. God has greater for me. In this stage you might struggle with consistency and at times you get off balance. Your feet might feel like that turtle stuck in peanut butter, but don't stop limping. You might have just accepted Christ today and are still facing some addictions and destructive behaviors so "don't get weary in well doing" (Galatians 6:9). You want to do it, you are trying to do it but you just can't quite succeed! Don't quit or give up because you are in the fight for your life.

It is important that you do not get comfortable in this stage. There are so many people who want to get to the final stage of leaping but fear holds them in the limping stage, the fear of the unknown. Because I have never walked, I have never been like the others around me. How do I live outside of my dysfunction? Here is a great acronym for *fear*; "false evidence appearing real." When you live your life in constant fear, you will never be able to live the life God has ordained for you to live. Just because you were born with a condition like the lame man does not mean you have to remain in that state of being.

You can be free and healed, but you have to just place one foot in front of the other. Before you know it, one step becomes two, then two steps become twenty and twenty becomes a hundred. All of a sudden you are no longer just limping but you are leaping.

Stage Two: LIFTING

> Therefore comfort each other and edify one
> another, just as you also are doing.
> (1 Thessalonians 5:11)

What you need is somebody stronger than you to help you get into position. In the second stage, the lifting, you surround yourself with people whose faith is greater than yours and start hijacking their faith. This means that you spend as much time as possible in the presence of people who understand the possibilities of faith. Faith is so vital to our Christian walk and deliverance that Hebrews 11:6 says that without faith, it is impossible to please God. Get rid of those friends who lack faith in God and in your journey to deliverance. When I was going through my challenge, I would get closest to that person crying out for God and deep in worship. I started trying to grab hold of their faith.

> ...but exhort one another daily, while it is
> called "Today," lest any of you be hardened
> through the deceitfulness of sin.
> (Hebrews 3:13)

You need people who will speak life to you and encourage you even when you seem to be limping still. They tell you "pull up those big girl panties or big boy boxers and get through this." They encourage your efforts instead of edifying your mistakes. Speak to yourself, "This is my year of change. I'm going to speak to things I've been living with and making do. I'm speaking to death, loneliness and fear." With every word you speak, you will receive more and more strength.

Stage Three: LEAPING

Peter and John offered the lame man a hand up instead of a hand out. When he received their assistance, he was able to stand and then leap into his destiny. God needed this man to prove to the local church folks who knew him since birth that He is a miracle worker. Can't you see them shouting to everyone, "Isn't that the lame man leaping who has been crippled since birth?" When deliverance is manifest, people start asking, "Isn't that the drug addict who lived down the street?" Can't you see them in wonderment praising God because no one could have accomplished this miracle but God! God wants to show out through your crazy praise.

If your finances are less than enough, pull out your checkbook and begin to speak life. Decree and declare that change is not only coming but it has arrived. Fear will not hold you hostage another day. The spirit of lack will no longer consume your thoughts. Rejection and abandonment will no longer control your relationships. I might get down, but I will rise again.

> We are hard-pressed on every side, yet
> not crushed; we are perplexed, but not in
> despair; persecuted, but not forsaken; struck
> down, but not destroyed.
> (2 Corinthians 4:8, 9)

I use the example of the lame man in describing those radical people who are the first at church, first to pray, first to worship and move when it's time to move. These are the ones who have been delivered from their past and realize they would not be where they are today except for God. Many people get stuck in their conformity and lose their zeal of God, however, when you have been pulled from the gates of hell, you become radical enough to do whatever it takes to stand! People with the worst pasts are crazy for Jesus.

> I beseech you therefore, brethren, by the
> mercies of God, that you present your
> bodies a living sacrifice, holy, acceptable to
> God, which is your reasonable service. And
> do not be conformed to this world, but be
> transformed by the renewing of your mind,
> that you may prove what is that good and
> acceptable and perfect will of God.
> (Romans 12:1-2)

As a result of what you're reading, I am expecting an onslaught of testimonials of miraculous change in your personal lives. Psalm 107:20 says that He sent His word and healed them and delivered them from their destructions.

You become what you think about most of the time. No longer will you be ruled by your emotions. Give God the authority to have rule and reign over your spirit, soul, body, heart, mind and will. Agree with me that your life will never be the same.

God is delivering you,
so no longer accept the cardboard
box people have put you in,
decorating it, and calling it home.

ten

Your Future is Calling

Living in Your Purpose

Let me conclude with telling you just how AWESOME our God really is. When you finally surrender your will to His, God has a way of giving you the most amazing surprises ever. Every day with Him is sweeter than the day before. I could have allowed my past to dictate my future. In fact, if I had gone with the world's statistics of what I should have become, today I would not have discovered my purpose and getting to love people back to life every single day. When *you* go through the worst of the worst, instead of regretting, *you* get busy living. God's possibilities meet your impossibility, then your life really becomes enjoyable.

The Journey to my Purpose

In 2011, I stopped focusing on the things I could not change. I began to spend more time with God in full pursuit of His plan for my life. I would just sit in His presence praying and weeping. I knew that my mind and my heart were changing. In this experience I learned, this is how a person receives the "Mind of Christ." His anointing was invading my life and thoughts like never before and I yearned for Him and to be in His presence.

It was in His presence I felt complete fulfillment. Spending this time in His presence God gave me a vision of my future and it was simply amazing. He showed me I was to become a force to be reckoned with. I began to recognize the purpose for my pain was for others and I had not suffered in vain. God was going to use every single thing I had experienced to pull so many out of the pit of darkness.

I became so excited knowing God was going to use me to complete such an audacious task. As a young girl I wanted to preach, but as an adult I wasn't so sure I could handle the daunting task of sermon preparation and delivery. After much prayer, I decided I was ready and gave God a resounding, Yes! I was ready to be the master's mouthpiece and snatch others out of hell just like He had done for me.

My mom and dad agreed to allow me to preach and wow, I was not as prepared as I thought. Nevertheless,

I did not let that minor setback deter me. I had made a commitment, God and I were more than willing to honor it. I started praying more, fasting and digging deeper into the Word. Finally, I became so confident in my ability. My parents allowed me another opportunity and I was more than ready. God moved so powerfully in that service. Lives were changed and so many people were set free.

Prior to becoming an itinerant minister, I feverishly posted on social media testifying of the amazing love of God. Before long I had maxed out my friends on Facebook, my twitter had more than 10,000 followers and Instagram was quickly picking up momentum.

What happened next is simply and only God. Invitations to minister began to come in and before long I was traveling twice a month, sometimes more, to preach and tell my story of healing. Although my first preaching engagement away from my local church was a bit terrifying, I felt like this was my purpose in life.

As I prepared to take on this new chapter, I began to cross examine myself. All the confidence I had once possessed was fading fast. "Was I ready? Could I speak in front of hundreds or thousands?" In this pivotal moment, I humbly asked God to help me. My simple prayer was, "Make me be the instrument God that You want to use for such a time as this." I then asked, "What could I say that would make a difference in a broken life?" Why were these people calling me, I still didn't know how to preach. I had not gone to seminary or been taught the hermeneutics of preaching. I had just made myself available to His will for my life and now God wanted to send me all over the world preaching, praying and prophesying life back into every person I would encounter. His response to my questioning was, "You be YOU. You follow me and I will open the windows of heaven over you."

When I ministered, God would wreck the place. Tears would begin flowing just at the sound of my voice. Immediately, I saw change in those who were attending my meetings. As I would be ministering, I would walk up to someone and begin to sing prophetically while hugging them. All of sudden, I could feel their pain leaving them. It was then I knew God had given me an anointing for hugging and loving people back to life. It was so life changing for me and I realized that hugs really do melt the pain away.

My desire to be in full time ministry suddenly became my passion. For five years I worked in retail cosmetics at Bloomingdale's. Although I knew my purpose was to be in full time ministry, it wasn't my time. I remained faithful to my secular job always doing my best until God said move. I had read in God's Word that those who are faithful in the little, He will reward them with much.

His lord said to him, 'Well done, good and
faithful servant; you have been faithful over
a few things, I will make you ruler over many
things. Enter into the joy of your lord.'
Matthew 25:23

Finally, I had found my calling
and purpose in life. Though it
didn't look like anything I had
ever seen, I was confidently
walking in it. I was watching God
literally restore everything in my
life. I was not only traveling to
minister but I was being asked to
speak on radio shows, television

GOD'S *POSSIBILITIES*
MEET YOUR
IMPOSSIBILITY
AND LIFE REALLY
BECOMES ENJOYABLE.

programs and prayer conference calls. Many of the
prayer conference calls were during the day around
noon. Because I was still working a fulltime job, on my
lunch hour I would go out to the parking lot and do
the prayer conference calls. Sitting there in my car, I
would pray the heavens down, and afterwards I would
go back inside and finish my shift. Never once did I feel
like God did not have His hand on exactly what was
unfolding in my life. The favor of God was so evident
in my life. Gradually my travel itinerary became more
and more hectic and the staff at Bloomingdale's worked
with me. They were on the front row watching God
elevate me and they were totally on board.

By the end of 2012, my social media sites had more than 250,000 followers. My strongest following came from Twitter, and then Instagram and Facebook. What so many had used for evil, God allowed me to use for good. I would communicate and share my own personal struggles that I had gone through and provided solutions to everyday problems faced in relationships and life. Throughout the day I would receive inbox messages from people saying they felt like I was in their room or in their prayer closet with them. People that had never heard of or even believed in Jesus, never gone to church were reaching out to me asking for prayer. God was enlarging my territories.

I did not make spectacular speeches, but God trusted me. I was consistent, I kept reminding myself that those who are faithful in the little, God will reward with much. I would travel to preach on weekends, fly home to lead worship on Sunday mornings at my church, and then go back to work at seven o'clock in the morning on Monday. I would be so tired however, I did it with a joyful heart because I KNEW God was doing something great, something I could not see and I simply trusted Him to do it.

It was an amazing journey as God took this girl who did not even minister at the first *Conquering Hell in High Heels™* Conference in 2011 and open doors around the world to minister at small, medium and mega churches as well as many conferences and conventions. In 2013,

God really began to enlarge my territory yet again. Almost every weekend I was traveling throughout the nation to preach, still leading praise and worship in my church and working forty hours a week. My annual conference had grown so substantially and explosively. After two years we had outgrown my church, and in 2014 we stepped out on faith and increased our capacity. It was an amazing testament of God's hand on my life and in the *Conquering Hell in High Heels* ministry. I knew that no one could stop something that God had endorsed.

On December 14, 2013, I was on my lunch break and heard the Holy Spirit say, "Turn in your two week notice NOW." I became SO excited. I passed the test of being faithful. I was committed to the process and I felt the release of something even greater about to happen. I was sad yet excited about closing this chapter in my life. After all, Bloomingdale's had been my home for 5 years and had become so dear to my heart. However, I had no doubt something even more exciting was about to happen and I was ready. I went through my divorce season there, my healing season there, and my advancement there. Nevertheless, I knew it was time to move.

January 1, 2014 was my first official day in full time ministry. On that day I recorded my first car video. I remember that day so vividly. Riding along in my car and hearing the Holy Spirit tell me to pull over and make a video. As I pulled my car over to the side of the road, I laughed much like Sarah when God promised her Isaac in her old age (Genesis 18:12). I picked up my cell phone and I began to record myself saying, "HELLO, AWESOME PEOPLE......" and I never imagined that tagline would be known all over the world. One ounce of obedience changed my whole life in an instant. Those *Car Chronicles,* as so many called them, went viral getting hundreds and some thousands of shares.

Yet again, my social media following exploded beyond my greatest expectation. By the end of February 2014, I was completely booked and 2015 was filling up as well. The 2014 *Conquering Hell in High Heels* Conference blew our minds and took my faith to a whole new level. We had people from all over the world in attendance and left totally set free and completely healed. Fast forward almost nine months later, I am writing the final chapter of my first book. Don't tell me that God isn't faithful.

THE TIDE IS TURNING AND EVERYTHING THAT HAS BEEN DRAINING YOU IS DRYING UP.

My patient obedient faithfulness to God and the plan he had for my life catapulted my ministry into a place far beyond where I ever envisioned it would go. Shortly after taking the leap of faith into full time ministry, I began my Tuesday morning prayer call. After just four weeks my staff was on the search to find a service that could handle the capacity of the prayer call. People were getting bumped or worse, they could not get through. My staff searched but could not find any service that would provide the capacity we needed. I explained to my callers the importance of getting on early and before time. So to secure a spot on the line, people literally started getting on 30 minutes early. Everything I was saying and doing was divinely designed and blessed by God. I could not and would not have done any of this without Him. He deserves all the glory for my successes thus far and beyond.

Maybe you are wondering why I am telling you all of this. Rest assured I am not boasting in my own strength and abilities, but solely in the power of God. I want to build up your faith and encourage you to use the broken pieces of your life to find your purpose. Like so many of you, the world had given up on me, counted me out, beaten me down, and seemingly taken everything from me. At 34, I had nothing and was forced to start all over again. The enemy thought he had won and I would never recover but look at me now. My life is better now than it has ever been.

At times it felt like God wasn't moving quickly enough, but God's time is not our time. His timing is perfect for Him and for me. He consistently proved His faithfulness to me and that He truly does restore time. Over these last few years, He proved to me that if I do my part He will do His. He has demonstrated to me and through my life that when He qualifies you, it doesn't matter if you dropped out of school, been divorced, made a million mistakes or been made to feel like biggest loser. God has the greatest redemption plan on the planet and He has written the greatest comeback story for your life. You must help God help you. Start by forgiving yourself, forgiving others and then wait on God's perfect timing. I am proof that God will show out in your life if you allow Him to have full access to your life.

Writing this book and looking back over my life, one thing I can tell you, I would not change anything except maybe making my mistakes earlier so I could get to this place a lot sooner. I would not trade one memory, one tear or one wrong choice that I have ever made. If I had to walk through the pain, the shame and the guilt again I would. Especially since I know how the story ends.

I have watched God restore my family. My sons and I can now reminisce and my heart no longer aches or becomes overwhelmed with guilt. They get to watch their mom love people back to life every day. They are so very proud of me and selflessly work in ministry alongside Mark, my parents and me. I have been given the greatest husband on the planet, Mark. This man loves me and my sons so effortlessly. He is so proud of the woman that I am becoming. His love has given me permission to let my quirky style come out and play.

He even lets me preach in tutus, Converse and he loves the crazy colored stripes I put in my hair. Mark loves and accepts everything about me. He loves all of me and I love all of him.

The landscape of my life has changed and developed so beautifully over the last eight years. I never thought I would have the incredible life I am living right now. There is so much peace within and I have learned to enjoy my parents. Their presence is a constant fixture and reminder of the gracious love of God. We live in the same neighborhood and I love doing ministry together with them. They have given me the space I needed to be who God has ordained and purposed me to be in this season of my life.

I didn't even know how to pray for all the blessings God has bestowed upon my life today. He has literally blown my mind and showed out on my behalf. Who could ever have imagined the life I would testify of today? I surely did not. Paul writes,

> But as it is written: "Eye has not seen, nor
> ear heard, nor have entered into the heart of
> man the things which God has prepared for
> those who love Him." (1 Corinthians 2:9)

I am so very thankful that I fearlessly chased after my healing and exposed my damaged heart to the greatest healer on the planet. I am grateful that I discovered the gift of goodbye in my healing process. Some people are assigned to you temporarily to provide life lessons and not for a lifetime attachment.

My final words to you are, I am moved with so much excitement about your future. I BELIEVE in you. I BELIEVE in the God who lives in YOU. Do your part! Become honest with yourself and let go of everything that's been holding you back. Don't be afraid to be vulnerable and transparent, healing is on the other side of letting it all out. Remember, just because it may be dark right now, it's not over. God had to turn off the lights to set up for your surprise party. Everything is turning around for you and working in your favor. Everything that has been draining you is drying up. IT'S A NEW SEASON!!!

Don't be afraid to be vulnerable and transparent, healing is on the other side of letting it all out.

Made in the USA
Middletown, DE
06 May 2018